Mind, Music & Imagery

Unlocking the Treasures of Your Mind

by

Stephanie Merritt, M.M., M.S.

Aslan

PUBLISHING

Published by
Aslan Publishing
3356 Coffey Lane
Santa Rosa, CA 95403
(707) 542-5400

Library of Congress Cataloging-in-Publication Data:

Merritt, Stephanie.
    Mind, music, and imagery : unlocking the treasures of
your mind / Stephanie Merritt. --1st ed.
            p.   cm.
    Includes bibliographical references (p. 253) and index.
    ISBN 0-944031-62-5
    1. Music, Influence of. 2. Self-actualization (Psychology)
3. Music--Physiological effect. 4. Music--Psychology.
5. Music therapy. I. Title.
MC3920.M43 1996
781'.11--dc20   95-43811
                                                              CIP
                                                              MN

Copyright ©1996 Stephanie Merritt

Cover Design by Steve Graydon
Page Design by Marianne Harris
Set in Bembo and Rage
Printed in the USA
Second Edition
First Edition published by Plume/Penguin Books

10 9 8 7 6 5 4 3 2 1

Music is a first cousin to teleportation—Listen and off you go—through the trees, riding the wings of the wind through kingdoms in the sky, skimming over the froth of the waves, bursting forth like a newborn star forming always anew the universe of creation....

—Audrey Graziani,
Music and Imaging Workshop Participant

Dedication

To my editor, Betty Deborah Ulius, for her unflagging faith in my work, her constant support, andher untiring efforts to help bring my years of research to fruition.

Acknowledgments

I would like to thank Dr. Helen Lindquist Bonny, founder of the Guided Imagery and Music (GIM) method, and the Association for Music and Imagery, whose guidance and expertise opened me up to the world inside me.

I am grateful to all the workshop participants, imagers, teachers and students who contributed their creative and unique imagery to this book.

And to Dr. Georgi Lozanov, my first great teacher, whose brilliance and humanitarian concept of education changed the direction of my life.

I would also like to thank Van Hutchinson and Hal A. Lingerman for their time and expertise in helping shape the final version of the manuscript. A special thanks to Myron Fink, composer and professor of music at Hunter College, for his invaluable assistance in compiling the music lists.

Dr. Helen Lindquist Bonny, Linda H. Keiser, Bonnie Fink, and Mark Ochu also read the manuscript in progress and offered insightful comments and support. Lynn May did a fine job of proofreading. Marilyn Clark not only read the manuscript but contributed her term "Music Imaging."

I am deeply grateful to Mary Ann Sowards for sharing her expertise in creative movement (included in Chapter 10 and Appendix B) and to Thomas Shanks, who selected, edited and mixed the music for the stories on the tape mentioned on the order form at the end of this book.

I would like to thank Audrey Graziani for her help with the exercises in Chapter 11, and Dave Dumanis for his patient and prolific editorial assistance. Thanks also to Linda Engstrom for her editorial expertise on this revised edition.

Forward by Robert Johnson

Music has always been a treasured companion to me in my life. I am in awe of its power to touch the soul and open the heart. When I listen to great music, I am in sacred space.

Imagery, too, is sacred. The images and symbols which emerge from the rich storehouse of the personal, as well as the collective, unconscious come to us when we need them, and assist us toward wholeness.

Both music and imagery speak the language of the unconscious, allowing us to make contact with the inner world. As a gateway to the images and symbols of the inner Self, music can bridge the gap between the conscious and the unconscious. it is a natural way to stimulate waking dreams and active imagination so that we can communicate with the unexplored or disowned parts of ourselves.

A book that helps us to understand that language and encourages us to experience the natural dialog between music and the rich treasures of the unconscious, is a book we will want to know. Stephanie Merritt's presentation is clear and simple, yet warm and inspirational. The musical activities at the end of each chapter offer the reader the opportunity to experience music's power to unleash imagination and creativity as well as its capacity to heal the psyche.

I first encountered Stephanie Merritt's work through a close friend, who often shared his Guided Imagery and Music journeys with me. Guided Imagery and Music (GIM) takes waking dreams and spontaneous imaging a step further by offering a container and framework in which symbols and images can manifest and, in the immediacy of music, shift and transform the energies of the psyche. I was fascinated by the quality and depth of the imagery the music was stimulating as my friend's personal myth unfolded. The music uncovered feelings and memories that had been buried, brought healing and catharsis, and evoked powerful archetypal material. My friend had profound insights that changed his life. The music allowed him to embrace his shadow, grieve his losses, and release the pain that had stored in his body.

Since this book was first published, many people have used its suggestions and activities to integrate the music of the Masters into their lives and, as a result, have experienced its transformative energies. Because of my own love for music and my dedication to imagery, I am delighted that so many others will benefit from their coming together in this potent synthesis.

About the Author

Stephanie Merritt has Masters Degrees in Counseling Psychology and Education, and is a psychotherapist in private practice in San Diego. She is the Director of the Southern California Center for Music and Imagery, and presents workshops and trainings internationally on self-development and creativity enhancement through music. She is a Fellow and Certified Trainer of the Association for Music and Imagery and offers all levels of training in the Bonny Method of Guided Imagery and Music..

She has taught at the University of San Diego and City University of Seattle, and the University of California at San Diego. She has served as training consultant for a new Accelerated Learning magnet school in the San Diego city school district. She was Academic Coordinator of the Lozanov Learning Institute of San Diego, having trained under the direction of pioneer educator, Georgi Lozanov of Bulgaria. She is the author of *Successful, Non-Stressful Learning*.

Currently she is using guided imagery and music for collective grief and for intercultural communication between diverse ethnic and national groups.

Preface

When *Mind, Music and Imagery* was first published in 1990, the field of mind/body medicine was just beginning to flourish. The concept of music as healer in the modern world was developing, and the impact of emotions on the health of the body was being explored and researched after a long period of mind/body split. Now, quantum scientists, and physicians such as Bernie Siegel and Deepak Chopra, have shown us that the body is more like music than it is like a machine. There is even speculation that DNA itself may be intrinsically musical. Healing vibration with vibration is beginning to make sense. The work of Jeanne Achterberg and others has shown imagery to be an important tool for healing, and music, as we are discovering, is a natural stimulator of imagery. As the mind/body connection is scientifically validated, more and more people are using music to heal their bodies.

In these last few years, music has also proved itself to be a unique and effective way to traverse the left/right brain gap into mental acuity and creative expression. New research at the University of California at Irvine has revealed that students achieve higher test scores with classical music, and researchers are concluding that the music may be stimulating the firing of neurons in the brain. People everywhere are studying and learning to music that can organize their thoughts and spark new ideas.

Psychologically, music is finally being recognized as a prime mover of blocked emotions and a direct, yet safe path to non-ordinary states of consciousness where we can access information and insights that can change our lives. The expressive arts therapies and, in particular, GIM (Guided Imagery and Music) are becoming a respected and highly recommended psychotherapy as people continue to experience immediate and transformational impact on their lives. GIM is now being used in hospitals, clinics and hospices around the U.S., as well as in private practice as a primary tool for healing and personal growth. It has also expanded, through the Association for Music and Imagery, to Europe, Australia, New Zealand, and other areas around the world.

Although GIM began as a way to explore non-ordinary states of consciousness and transpersonal states, it has proved to be an invaluable tool for clinical work in psychotherapy. In the five years since this book was published, I have used GIM very successfully in my psychotherapy practice for depression, anxiety, grief and loss, addiction recovery, creativity, and personal and spiritual growth. GIM has also impacted the healing process of people with AIDS, severe arthritis, cancer, and other illnesses.

I have seen people transform their lives as the music brings out their inner strengths and resources, and empowers them. I continue to be humbled by the wholeness and wisdom that lie within each one of us, just waiting to be awakened by a musical herald. Each day, I become more convinced that therapists can not know what their clients need, but the clients themselves know, on some level, exactly what will heal them. My work, as a therapist, is to help them discover this inner knowing through music, my co-therapist. I've also come to understand the important role of the transpersonal in healing body, mind and spirit. GIM does not just solve people's problems nor does it focus on pathology. It enables them to see themselves as spiritual beings with endless possibilities.

In the past few years, I have been giving workshops and seminars in Europe. Through my work in Germany and Austria with adult children of war, I am becoming aware of the power of music and imagery to tap into the collective grief inside each one of us. Our personal grief seems inexorably linked with the grief of our nation, and even our world. Music may be a powerful enough container to hold that grieving space, enabling us to acknowledge the pain and release the energy needed to move toward global peace and unity.

With the growing trend toward mainstream use of music for healing, creativity and spiritual growth, this book may be even more significant than ever. The first edition of *Mind, Music and Imagery* brought me letters from around the world from people whose lives had been enriched simply by listening to some of the music selections I recommended, and doing the suggested exercises. I have chosen to revise the New Age music list on page 94, simply because some of the original selections are outdated, and there are many wonderful new pieces available.

It is my hope that all the mental health professionals, educators, and individual music lovers who have used this book with substantial results, will continue to find inspiration, insight and guidance in these pages, and that new readers will discover for themselves the richness that great music can bring to their lives.

Table of Contents

Music Activities Table of Contents

Chapter Seven: The Rhythm of Emotion

Chapter Eight: Music and the Multiple Brain/Mind

Chapter Nine: The Uncharted Unconscious

Chapter Ten: Taking Learning Off the Page

Chapter Eleven: Unmasking Your Secret Self

Authors Note:

I believe that language is a powerful tool, and that the way we use it can influence us below the threshhold of consciousness. I am particularly aware of the subtle psychological effect of using the generic "he" or "him" to indicate persons of either sex or both sexes. At the same time, I find it awkward to use he/she or him/her, as it often interferes with the flow of communication.

Until we invent a new form that is comfortable for all of us, one that honors both sexes, I have chosen to use both masculine and feminine pronouns alternately.

Empowering Yourself Through Music

Music is a moral law. It gives a soul to the universe, wings to the mind,
flight to the imagination, a charm to sadness, gaiety and life to everything.
It is the essence of order, and leads to all that is good, just and beautiful.

–Plato

Imagine a child, bright and wide-eyed. Look into her eyes and notice the mixture of daring, sparkle and light-hearted innocence. Touch her face and feel her soft skin. All her movements are effortless and lithe; her eager mind reaches out for her next adventure.

If you could magically enter her mind, you might discover an enchanted world of princesses, kings and queens, witches, wise old men, and talking frogs. You might see places you have never seen with your outer eye: bewitched castles and cottages, a forest of talking trees, meadows filled with dancing figures in gossamer white gowns.

Imagine yourself descending into ever deeper levels of this child's mind. Feel yourself being immersed in her world of fantasy, in the brilliance of its colors, the richness of its lands and people, the fullness of feeling they stir up in you. "But this is not real," you say to yourself. And yet you feel more alive here than in all the real places you've been in.

You now hear the soft strains of a flute and harp concerto coming from this child-mind. The incoming pulses of music energy begin to form a pattern, to take on the vague form of a flower. As it enters her mind, she imbues it with color. She feels those velvety petals with the fingertips of her mind and smells their fragrance. All the images, feelings and memories she has ever associated with flowers come out of their hiding places to connect with this new flower. Ideas begin to pop like ripe seed-pods from the electrical connections these patterns are making; thousands of them all at once.

Suddenly she shouts with pleasure at her newest insight: she herself is that flower. She feels the softness of her petals and the strength of her stem. She feels herself blossoming. And she knows at that moment that everything she will ever learn about the growth of a flower will be accompanied by the hundreds of thousands of pictures, feelings, sounds and smells that dwell together in her inner reality.

You stand there inside her mind, awed by the vibrant energy of those images. But even as they give you pleasure, you may feel another emotion, a sadness at your own loss of communication with the world within yourself. This child still has the gift of vivid memory and creative insight, and you hope that she will never lose the freshness of her youthful vision.

There is an inner reality. *There is a world inside our minds that is as valid as, if not more valid than, the world outside us.* Poets and prophets have spoken of its existence for eons, but to many educators this is a strange and unacceptable concept. And our teachers pass that concept on to us. How often have you heard someone say, "It's just your imagination," or "You're only imagining that," as though the world of imagination and feeling were not quite valid? Although we are entering an era that emphasizes personal growth and spiritual transformation far beyond our old parameters, we are still in a transition stage. Our left-brained, reductionist way of thinking makes us believe that if we can't see, touch, or manipulate something, it is not real and has no significance in our lives. But if we are, as Fritjof Capra and other quantum physicists profess, patterns of energy waves constantly in motion, then it follows that we would be influenced by other vibrational patterns around us. According to psychologist Marion Woodman,

> *Something is happening on a large scale—there are radical changes in male-female relationships, and there is an enormous interest in spirit and matter in the fields of science, psychology, and biology. I think many people are doing a lot of inner work; they are really trying to understand what is going on inside themselves.* [1]

This book is an invitation to walk in a land that may be unfamiliar to you, but may awaken you to new ways of being with yourself and those around you. It is designed to widen the scope of what we normally think of as learning to embrace the development of our whole beings. Learning to know ourselves and our world, whether in or out of the classroom, involves the relaxation of our bodies, the focusing of our minds, the unimpeded flow of our emotions, and the energy and perspective of our spiritual life. Through the healing and transforming energies of music and the images it evokes, learning becomes a full, rich, natural experience in which every aspect of our being is able to participate.

This book has been written particularly for those who may have little or no experience with music and its potential as a catalyst for personal growth.

A Musical Mind-Journey

Meaningless music is to the mind what unhealthy food is to the body. We often use music indiscriminately, with little or no awareness of how it might be affecting us.

We are becoming more aware of the importance of eating nutritious foods. Yet we may not know what to "eat" for our psychological digestion. We hear music around us everywhere: in restaurants and department stores, in exercise gyms and art galleries. We hear it so much, in fact, that we often do not notice it. We take it for granted. We become immune to it—even numb to its presence. As I was leaving a restaurant with a friend, I remarked how beautiful the classical guitar music had been during the meal. My friend said, "What music?"

I have taught hundreds of Music Imaging workshops, and the capacity of music to enhance learning and personality development, intellectual development, and health and well-being, has often astonished me. I have experienced this most profoundly in my own life. I have noticed that music has helped me to slow down my own inner rhythms. Whenever I feel them racing, I turn on some music that will balance me, and I feel good again. I have learned which music can lift me up and which music can help me descend into solitude.

There was a difficult time in my life when I felt victimized by everyone and everything around me. Although I had been raised on classical music (my mother was a fine pianist and also sang in the Boston Symphony choir under Charles Munch at Tanglewood), I had not been aware that I could use it intentionally to bring myself into balance, to help me resolve life issues, and to integrate neglected aspects of my psyche. Using imagery and music, I dug through layers of repressed angers, guilts, sorrows and buried joy to unearth strengths and talents I never knew I had. Once up to the surface and accessible, I could use these emotions to realize the potential that is my natural birthright. Music has empowered me.

My method of teaching is an amalgam of my training in stress-free, accelerated learning under the direction of psychotherapist and pioneer educator Dr. Georgi Lozanov of Bulgaria, the Guided Imagery and Music (GIM) technique developed by Dr. Helen Lindquist Bonny, founder of the Institute for Music and Imagery, and my own vision of how music can be used to enhance learning, gained through many years of experience in my field.

I was led to Dr. Bonny and her GIM method through my work with Dr. Lozanov. My experience with him changed my whole life. In 1979 I was teaching Spanish, and English as a Second Language. I found the process of teaching adults to actually speak a foreign language long, tedious and frustrating.

Dr. Lozanov, who developed a system of accelerated, stress-free learning, taught me how to teach people to speak basic conversational Spanish in 24 sessions. We used classical music, games, songs and drama to make learning a successful, joyful experience.

As I taught class after class, I began to realize that many of my students were making major shifts in their personalities. Shy, inhibited students came out of their shells; aggressive students softened and began to relate to others more sociably. Many people discovered that they could be creative, imaginative, spontaneous and intuitive. They simply had never been encouraged to develop these qualities.

I blossomed as well. I began to write songs designed to help students learn; I discovered that I could be very funny in the classroom. I seemed to be able to tune into the spirit of the moment and spontaneously do the right thing.

Dr. Lozanov's smiling eyes and gentle ways taught me to communicate to students that learning is a natural, holistic process which involves much more than abstract reasoning. Evalina Gateva, Dr. Lozanov's assistant, taught us Italian in three weeks. She demonstrated, through her high energy, body language, voice tone and use of music that, when all three layers of the brain and both hemispheres are activated, and when the conscious and unconscious minds are integrated, the end result is a phenomenal learning experience. This type of integrated learning reaches what Dr. Lozanov calls "the reserve capacities of the mind."

I noticed that the music played in class seemed to put people back in touch with the full potential of their true nature, although at the time I had no idea of how it was doing that.

I also noticed in these sessions that, even as the music seemed to be integrating the various aspects of the individual student, it was also connecting the minds and hearts of these individuals into a sense of identity as a group: the students developed a sense of family. They were caring and helpful to each other. This attitude contrasted starkly with the competitive corporate world many of them dealt with every day.

Through Dr. Lozanov and his pioneering work in education I began to experience my own expansiveness and that of my students. I continue to push back my limits through a more conscious approach to music, and its vital connection to the mind and spirit.

What Music and Imagery Can Do For You

In my Music Imaging workshops I have seen people blossom in remarkable ways. The Music Imaging you will learn in this book can do many things for you:

- It can lower your stress level and promote healing
- It can open you up to aspects of yourself you have never encountered: the risk-taker, the playful child, the free spirit.
- It can give you a different perspective on your life and empower you to resolve inner conflicts and overcome obstacles.
- It can enrich your life and expand your world by its sheer beauty.
- It can increase your learning and memory retention.
- It can stimulate your creativity and imagination
- If you are a parent, you can use special Music Imaging activities to stimulate your own as well as your children's imaginations. Many parents have found that this "quality time" not only opens up communication between themselves and their children, but also strengthens their children's self image.
- It can relax, renew and soothe you.

Workshop participants have often told me they will never listen to music in the same way again. Here are a few responses to the experience of conscious listening. Corry McKissack of Monrovia, California, remarked:

> *"As an incurable skeptic, I have to admit I was amazed at what can be done with your approach to music and the way you utilize it in opening*

up the inner self and the avenue to becoming a more whole person, in order to be able to unfold unknown abilities within us."

Here are the comments of Tim DeWeese of Pomona, California:

"This workshop was especially helpful in restoring motivation for me, plus inspiration, peace, imagination and spiritual awakening."

Marilyn Bock, a teacher in Chugiak, Alaska, wrote:

"I had introduced Classical and Baroque music into vocabulary study of Latin prefixes in English class. Other classes heard about this experience and asked me if they could listen to "my" music during work sessions. They have reported the disappearance of headaches and weariness. Personally, I have used several of Mozart's pieces during resting sessions to promote healing of lower back strain. My family and my students have responded extremely positively to the healing energies of music."

As you can see, each of these workshop participants had a different need: the first wanted to become a "more whole person" and unfold her unknown abilities; the second wanted to restore motivation; the third used it to release stress, for herself as well as her students. For all three, and many others, learning how to use music and imagination enriched their lives.

In addition to my workshops, I also work on a one-to-one basis, using the Guided Imagery and Music method. Dr. Helen Bonny developed and researched GIM at the Maryland Psychiatric Center. It has been successful with substance abusers, psychiatric inpatients and physically ill patients, as well as with healthy persons seeking personal growth and a higher level of creativity. GIM is a method of self-exploration in which a person listens to specially programmed classical music in a relaxed state, allowing images and feelings to come to awareness. The listener or "traveler" shares these images with a guide while the music is playing. Rather than providing a background, the music is an active agent. It may evoke visual images, feelings, memories, colors, fragrances, sounds or kinesthetic responses. After the music has ended, the "traveler" shares insights

about the images and their connection to her current life issues. The
GIM experience may then be expressed through drawing, creative writing or other artistic media.[2]

I recently spoke to a client with whom I had worked a year ago. I
had done a series of six GIM sessions with her. She is a very creative,
right-brained person who had difficulty organizing her time, expressing
her thoughts in words, and working with numbers. I asked her to write
to me and let me know if the sessions had made a difference in her life.
This is what she wrote:

> *I began a series of GIM sessions in the hope that it would help me find a
> way to bring about an integration of left and right hemispheric brain func-
> tion.*
>
> *The GIM facilitator and I discussed the situation and decided to set
> three intentions: first, to explore what happens in the dominant right hemi-
> sphere; then to move into the left hemisphere and gather information it might
> present; and. finally, to ask for an appropriate and pleasurable functional
> integration of the two brain hemispheres.*
>
> *In a relaxed, trustful state, I followed my guide's voice as she led me to
> the place where the music began.*
>
> *In the right brain experience, there was a feeling of euphoria as a little
> sprite/smoky wisp arose in rhythm with the music, twirling and swirling,
> soaring into vast realms where free flight and beautiful colors interchanged
> continuously and effortlessly. The light was incredibly bright. There was per-
> fect joy and freedom, with no desire to do anything other than continue mov-
> ing farther and farther out.*
>
> *My trip into the left hemisphere stopped at the threshold. It was so
> dark, I didn't want to continue. I could sense that the area was filled with
> machines and filing cabinets of extremely heavy metal and wood. There was
> no way to move through the overwhelmingly oppressive heaviness, rigidity
> and cold darkness there.*
>
> *These impressions very vividly and accurately expressed my dilemma in
> a way that I could feel with my whole being. I was reluctant to believe that a
> resolution for this problem could be found in my psyche, but was so curious
> that I wanted to "be there" if something presented itself. I trusted the GIM
> process and the ability and integrity of my guide. Together we approached the*

final intention: integration.

We set both hemispheres in motion simultaneously, the right brain sprite whirling farther and farther away; the left brain becoming more remote. And then I heard a "still. small voice" say, "We came here to integrate these two. Now is the time!"

My attention shifted to the left hemisphere and stopped there, unable to proceed. But suddenly the little sprite appeared and flew into the darkness. Everywhere it went, windows opened and light began to shine out: it worked gracefully and joyously, letting light and air flow into the musty, forbidden places. Soon my body felt completely relaxed. I began to discover all the words. numbers and expressions being released by the heart and soul of the little right-brained sprite. I felt a connection, a coming together, as a bridge was built for the communication/traffic to flow in both directions.

Now, whenever I need to write a report or teach a class, I pause to re-experience that moment in my mind-body, moving into the task at hand with a sense of security, expectation and wonder, knowing that both hemispheres are working together on the project.

Another woman I worked with found her life much freer after 18 GIM sessions. At 54, with two children and several grandchildren, Meg's life was still being run by her mother. Having come from a family with a history of alcoholism and drug abuse, Meg was putting enormous amounts of energy into rebelling against her mother's idea of who she should be. In one GIM session, she imaged herself as a square wooden peg trying to fit into a round hole. On a physical and emotional level, she experienced the struggle of trying to fit. No matter how hard she tried, she just could not get that peg into the hole. Finally, she decided to withdraw it, and sand it down a little to make it rounder and softer.

As she stopped trying to fit into the hole, the hole closed up and disappeared. The peg became less angular and more curvy. The next week, this woman, who always looked rather austere and not very feminine, who never wore make-up, came in to her session wearing make-up and a beautiful, feminine outfit. She looked softer and lovelier than I had ever seen her look. She was no longer living just to show her mother she was no China doll in black patent shoes.

Before she could make this breakthrough, she needed to confront and contend with her "shadow" aspects and bring them out of hiding. The music of Bach, with its primal power, allowed her to be in her own darkness for awhile to look at those parts of herself she had never allowed to surface. One such image took the shape of a chicken gizzard in her stomach. She had had stomach aches all her life and never understood the cause. Letting herself feel the ugliness and repulsiveness of this chicken gizzard and noticing the pain it caused led her to recognize it as a symbol of her own anger about her mother's suffocating protectiveness. This resentment had lain, all those years, like a lump in her stomach.

When she embraced her wounds by acknowledging them, she was able to bring herself into balance, healing her relationship with her mother and moving into wholeness herself. This inner process was reflected in her outer life. She evidenced new vitality, presence, and a sense of relaxation as if she had finally cut the umbilical cord. A year later, she still feels the effects of this psychic shift in her sense of inner strength and autonomy. Writing on the effect of GIM on her life, she said:

It gave me an opportunity to see myself as a child. I was very lonely and never quite understood what was expected of me. It made me sad when I was small, and rebellious when I was older. It became clear that my mother loved me very much, but as a possession, not really as a person. She was more concerned with the package than what was in it. She wasn't able to separate her identity from mine, and this has continued to be confusing for us both. I am becoming less resentful as I see she did the best she could: her smothering type of mothering was all she knew. I am also not so hard on myself for what I perceive as my inherited failures as a mother.

Given my background and the era in which I lived, my children got the best I could give them at the time. I may not have known how to love them in an unconditional way, but I am able to work on that now. It also seems possible that someday I will be able to love my mother in an unconditional way. The chicken gizzard that inhabits my stomach is shrinking, and barely recognizable most of the time. My trash can of internal garbage no longer overflows. I resisted the temptation to settle for a renewal of an old relationship with my ex-husband. I was able to look at what I wanted and needed

in a loving relationship—and see that the negatives outweighed the positives.
The only person I can change is MYSELF!

Composing Your Journey

The journey we will be taking together through music and your imagination will provide you with a vital tool for self-development. You will become an active creator of your own sound environment, rather than being at the mercy of every hammering rock video and grating aspirin commercial that invades your quieter moments. You will learn that you need not be a slave to the stresses of our high-tech society. If you feel tense and harried, you can release that tension with just a few minutes of calming music. If you are depressed, you don't need to stay depressed. A short sound-bath in certain kinds of music will lift you out of your depression. And if you feel alone, you need only to walk over to your stereo and turn it on. You may find in the music a friend and companion, an inner voice that seems to sense what you need and which path you should take, a Divine Presence that lets you know you are being protected and guided.

Taking control of your sound environment is an essential part of taking control of your life: you will learn to be your own composer, composing precisely the right conditions for your inner self to flourish.

Music can assist you in *letting your feelings flow.* When conditions seem too frightening to let out your feelings, you can invite music's gentle nudge to help you express them. As you allow the music to help you experience pain and sadness, all the locked-up joy bursts forth too, releasing a vitality that kindles interest and excitement in all aspects of your life: your work, your relationships, your studies. You reconnect with that child-like sense of wonder you lost in the traumas of early childhood, and, with a child's sense of wonder, you will feel truly alive.

Embracing your inner child releases the spontaneous creativity you may have hidden away with your old story books and broken toys. As you make music and imagery an integral part of your experience, you are empowered to transform your life in new and exciting ways.

Learning how to learn with music and imagery expands your learning experience and that of your children by encompassing several levels of consciousness and integrating them, so that learning becomes what it was meant to be: a natural, joyful, rich experience. We will explore the results of a humane and holistic way of learning and how it helps both children and adults awaken to their inner strengths and deeper promptings, and to integrate these qualities into their life experience.

Music can *unlock the doors to the full potential of your creativity.* We will look at the different genres of music to discover which ones are most effective for writing a poem or an essay, learning a foreign language, or working on your psychological process. Various musical suggestions will be offered for different purposes, and you will be guided into choosing appropriate music for each activity. With five easily available musical selections, you can begin your musical travels into your mind, your feelings and your spirit. Who knows what new or ancient aspects of yourself you may find in these inner realms?

No Experience Necessary

In presenting my workshops, I have found that comparatively few people have classical music in their homes. Perhaps this is because their parents were unaware of the psychological value of this music, and they have grown up believing it to belong to the province of the traditionalists and stuffed shirts of the world, or people of a more intellectual nature. Another reason might be that it is not casual background music, but music that reaches into the psyche and asks the listener to respond. It could simply be that the person has not been exposed to classical music, doesn't know what he or she would like, and hesitates to go into a record store and confront walls of unfamiliar recordings.

Many parents express concern about the effects of contemporary popular music on their youngsters, but don't know what to replace it with. Classical music is as potent as ever, and it is vitally relevant to today's consciousness. Today, a Beethoven symphony still evokes the same euphoria and spiritual insight as it did a century ago, but now we need it more than Beethoven himself could have imagined.

You don't have to know a lot of facts about classical music in order to feel its impact. There are some basic differences between the various types of classical music, and I give suggestions throughout this book as to how and when you might use each kind.

Begin by listening with your heart and an open mind. You will be amazed at the secrets the music holds within it, and its power to communicate to each individual in a unique way.

Music Activity #1
Music and Goals

You have started on the path to unearthing the treasures of your mind. The following list lays out some common motivations for taking this path. Check the list and grade the importance of each statement, 1 through 10. You might be surprised to discover which of them really matter to you most:

- I want to become more creative
- I want to break through emotional blocks
- I want to connect with that place of stillness deep inside me
- I need to find a way to feel relaxed and refreshed in a short period of time
- I want to learn to balance my emotions in order to function more fully
- I would like to discover my own inner guidance to help me resolve life issues
- I don't want to be numb anymore; I want to feel joy again
- I am overly serious and would like to give the child in me a chance to come out and play
- I dislike mundane tasks, and need to find something that will motivate me to do them

○ I want to use music as a vehicle to connect me with my spiritual source

○ I need to focus on my work or my studies without getting distracted or tired

○ I would like to learn which musical selections will energize me in the morning, calm me at bedtime and release my tensions during the day

○ I want to use music and imagery to enrich my relationships

○ I want to teach my children how to get in touch with their feelings and stimulate their imaginations

○ I want to stimulate my whole brain and integrate my conscious and unconscious mind

○ I want to make peace with my past

○ I want to get in touch with my full potential

○ I have put myself in a box and I want to break out of it

As you get further into learning how to use music, you may find that your priorities have changed, and some statements at the bottom of the list are now finding their way to the top. Once you start to use it regularly, music can clear your mental computer circuits and permit you to see clearly your paramount goals.

Music Activities

There are several music activities for every chapter in this book. They are simple, practical exercises designed to allow you to apply the essence of each chapter in your life. In order to do all the activities in the book you will need certain things:

1. Many of the activities are done to music. For simplicity's sake, I have chosen five easily available musical selections that are used throughout the text. They are:

J. S. Bach   Brandenburg Concerto No. 1
(You may substitute any of the other five Brandenburg Concertos)
Debussy   *Prelude to the Afternoon of a Faun*
Mozart   *Eine Kleine Nachtmusik*
Pachelbel   Canon in D
Vivaldi   *The Four Seasons*

2. You will need a journal big enough to draw in, and a pen, pastels or crayons.

3. You will also need a quiet room with a comfortable place to relax. Use floor pillows, a couch, bed or futon. An uncluttered corner of the room in which you place plants, flowers, rocks, shells, crystals or other aesthetic objects will help you feel your connection to nature and the universe.

Keeping a Journal

Many of the Music Activities call for you to write in your journal, draw, or do both. I have found that keeping a journal of my own music listening experiences becomes a concrete indicator of my personal and spiritual growth. It is fascinating to look back eight months later, and note the changes in the way I think, in the way I perceive life, in my relationships, and in my goals. A journal is a visible indicator of the growth of your understanding, and quickly becomes a valued companion.

Working with music and imagery is like dreaming when you're awake. You may find yourself in an altered state of consciousness. During this time, many insights, memories and creative ideas may occur to you. Unless we pay attention to them, they fly away. Just as we can integrate much valuable dream material when we write down our dreams, we can integrate our unconscious promptings, desires, fears and angers into our consciousness when we write down the impressions that music evokes. Writing honors and makes concrete our inner experience.

Just as you look through an old photograph album and say, "Did I look like that?" the journal is a mirror of your inner journey. In looking over her journal from the last year, a client of mine, who had done a series of Guided Imagery and Music sessions, and who had recovered from a deep depression, could not believe the changes in her energy and outlook. In addition to her writing, she also drew mandalas after each session. The changes in her psyche were graphically depicted in her mandalas.

Drawing With Music

Drawing, because it is non-verbal, can have even more impact than writing. You may draw on a blank sheet of paper, or first draw a circle on the paper and use the circle as a structure for a mandala. The mandala is an ancient, eternal symbol which has no beginning or end, and reveals the progress of the psyche. Always listen to the music first, in a relaxed state. When the music has ended, draw the images the music brought you. If they are significant to you, hang up the drawings in your room.

Music Activity #2
Response to Conscious Listening

You will need 30 minutes for this next activity. The purpose of this activity is to show you that all classical music does not have the same effect on you. How you feel when you hear Bach may be very different from your response to Debussy.

o Make yourself comfortable.

o Turn on each of the five selections above.

o Listen to about five minutes of each selection.

o Notice how each one makes you feel. No need to analyze. Relax and let your body and emotions tell you what they feel.

o Note in your journal or on this page how each piece made you feel. If the piece stirred up your emotions, note in the comments section which emotions it aroused.

J.S. Bach, *The Brandenburg Concerto No. 1*
(second movement)

⇨ Did the music calm you?

⇨ Did it energize you?

⇨ Did it put you in a dream-like state?

⇨ Did it stir up your emotions?

⇨ Did it focus your mind?

Comments:

Debussy, *Prelude to The Afternoon of a Faun*
➪ Did the music calm you?
➪ Did it energize you?
➪ Did it put you in a dream-like state?
➪ Did it stir up your emotions?
➪ Did it focus your mind?
Comments:

Mozart, *Eine Kleine Nachtmusik*
➪ Did the music calm you?
➪ Did it energize you?
➪ Did it put you in a dream-like state?
➪ Did it stir up your emotions?
➪ Did it focus your mind?
Comments:

Pachelbel, Canon in D
➪ Did the music calm you?
➪ Did it energize you?
➪ Did it put you in a dream-like state?
➪ Did it stir up your emotions?
➪ Did it focus your mind?
Comments:

Vivaldi, *The Four Seasons* (Spring Section)
➪ Did the music calm you?
➪ Did it energize you?
➪ Did it put you in a dream-like state?
➪ Did it stir up your emotions?
➪ Did it focus your mind?
Comments:

Notes

1. Kisly, Lorraine, "An Interview with Marion Woodman." Parabola, Vol. XII, No. 2, May 1987.

2. For more information on *Guided Imagery and Music* (GIM), contact The Southern California Center for Music and Imagery (SCCMI), P.O. Box 230386, Encinitas, CA 92024, or the Association for Music and Imagery (AMI), c/o James Ramkin, 331 Soquel Avenue, Suite 201, Santa Cruz, CA 95062-2331.

Finding Your Feelings

Music is a wonderful way to connect with your feelings. You can begin by noticing the impact of music on your emotions as you listen at home. Even more beneficial is Music Imaging in a group setting with a facilitator. Working in a group with a professional imaging guide not only provides permission to feel, but offers the added dimension of a unique group dynamic. The music connects the minds and hearts of the participants, and results in a bonding which opens them up to each other in a magical way. A psychiatrist attending a Music Imaging workshop was amazed to observe that total strangers were willing to share their most intimate thoughts and feelings with each other.

At a workshop focusing on Music Imaging for stress management, one of the women in the group had a revelation that changed the course of her marriage. In ten minutes of Debussy's Sacred and Profane Dances, she saw herself walking through a dark, brambly forest with her husband. They were neither talking nor touching each other. She came to the sudden jolting realization that that was how her marriage had been for years: non-communicative. At that point in her imagery, she and her husband came out of the forest into a light and sunny clearing. They were holding hands and speaking to each other in tender voices. As tears streamed down her face, the woman shared this experience with the group.

She told us that she hadn't cried in a very long time. Her marriage had been joyless, but her feelings had been so numbed that she had never realized it. That night, she phoned her husband and spoke to him from her heart. He responded the same way, sharing his anxiety at having just turned fifty. The experience was an awakening that opened up channels of communication for them both.

Opening Up With Music

Author George Leonard, who explores the rhythm of relationship in his book *The Silent Pulse,* says that even an ordinary conversation between two people is like a dance: a non-verbal rhythmic interaction that brings the listener into oneness with the speaker. Singing or marching together can synchronize breathing, and synchronized heartbeats are common among psychologists and their clients.

In a musical performance, the members of an orchestra must become as one. Leonard observes that:

> *We have become accustomed to such miracles: the extraordinary faculty of jazz musicans to "predict" precise pitch and pattern during improvisation, the simultaneous sweep of sixty bows in a symphony orchestra. The miracle springs not so much from individual virtuosity and sectional pyrotechnics as from the ability of a large group of human beings (hundreds, in oratorios) to sense, feel, and move as one.*[1]

Certain music seems to create an environment of trust and openness that allows the listeners to bare their souls and shed their encumbrances. At another workshop, a colleague of mine who had attended—supposedly just to observe—wrote a poem that deeply affected the group. She had been a writer for many years, yet she rarely shared her personal feelings with anyone. The poem was written, she said, almost without conscious

thought, as fast as she could fill the page, to the second movement of the
Bach *Brandenburg Concerto No. 5:*

> *I think of those whom I have loved*
> *Who've gone before me into the light.*
> *My smiling mother, my father who*
>   *could never pass an ice cream store*
>   *without leaving his mark.*
>
> *My loves—all three—so different:*
> *Ted of the sea-gray eyes and New England ways,*
> *Theo, who healed all he ever touched,*
> *Lenny, who made films and died of it.*
> *And my sister, hard and generous,*
>   *with a mouth that could laugh*
>   *and a tongue that could kill.*
>
> *And—in my self-imposed isolation—*
>   *my cat children:*
> *Samantha, blue-eyed, my familiar, my friend,*
> *And Angel, who I could not give away as a kitten*
>   *because she sat on my shoe and looked at me*
>   *as though I were her world.*
>
> *All gone, gone into the light.*
>
> *But life is a dance—like an English round.*
> *We form a circle and touch and smile*
> *and feel each other's warmth.*
> *And then it's over—that circle—*
> *And we must touch other hands and*
>   *smile into other eyes.*
> *Until we too go into the light.*
>
> *And that's called life.*

In ten minutes of music, this writer, who claimed she had never written in this spontaneous way before, saw all of the major losses in her life

pass before her. She allowed herself to feel these losses and to express them. As the sadness was felt, it resolved itself into an acceptance of the ephemeral nature of relationship and of life. This experience freed her to move on beyond her grief.

Even in a short Music Imaging workshop, the music helps people to bring forth deeply buried feelings. The following poem was written to a Bach concerto in less than 20 minutes by a Doug Child, a 28-year-old man who had only written one other poem in his life:

A shell on the beach...a conch.
Never have I felt such dryness.
A final farewell to this old shell,
Sliding out of it like a last slide down
The banister of the old house.

Sand...dry this time, not like
At the bottom of the sea.
Footprints in the sand being washed away
By the surging tide.
I'm sorry to see them go because they're
My first footprints.
They lead me to the old pier, its encrusted
Pilings wearing their living skins
Of mussels and moss

These new feet take me to the grassy tussocks
At the beach's edge.
I lay on my back.
Hearing the ocean that I had felt,
Feeling the breezes I'd never heard of.
Clouds float by,
And I remember the kelp beds
Swaying in the tide.

A soft-spoken, reserved woman, who is a teacher, allowed the music to help her to explore her feelings of sexual passion:

Smooth, gray, cool
A warm band of yellow through the gray
Swirls of white
Touch me.
I am larger than you can imagine.
Come inside me.

But it's so dark.
No, I'm opening up for you
Light is coming in now.
See me!

So intricate you are!
I feel as though I'm in a maze.
But no, you've shown me right where I am.
I see this part of you.
I understand.

Here, this part has been crusted over.
It is a hard crust.
I want to see what you have in this compartment.

No, not yet.
I myself cannot even remove that crust.

Maybe together we can.
Oh, but look. Here is another lovely part of you!
And here you are living flesh still.
Look, the flesh of you is growing, and growing!

It's because you are here in me now.
I was almost dead.

These poems, written without forethought or critical analysis, seemed to spontaneously flow out of a space we rarely allow ourselves to inhabit: a deeply expressive, hidden niche where long-forgotten feelings still live, along with the memories that gave birth to them. Each poem expresses, metaphorically, powerful subconscious feelings of which the poet may not be aware. Music gently prods and pries these feelings out of their hiding places until they willingly burst forth, uncensored, onto a piece of paper. The release of these feelings then leaves a wide open space for a sense of joy or freedom to move in.

Guided Imagery and Music

Music Imaging is the term I use to describe Dr. Helen Bonny's method of *Guided Imagery and Music* (GIM) when it is used in a group setting. It is usually done in a workshop with a trained GIM facilitator. After a simple induction to relax the body and focus the mind, participants listen, in a relaxed state, to one or two selections from the GIM tapes, noticing the images that come up. Afterwards, a facilitator encourages them to draw or write, and share their images with each other. An adaptation of the process may be done at home without a facilitator. (See Music Activity #3, p. 46).

A personal GIM session is yet another way to connect with your feelings. It involves a longer, more in-depth exploration of feeling states, and requires a trained GIM practitioner or guide who interacts with the traveler. After inducing relaxation and focus, the guide plays an entire GIM tape, consisting of 30-45 minutes of different selections of music. The traveler is instructed to talk about the images the music evokes.

Guided Imagery and Music is not the same as Guided Imagery. Although both methods tap the unconscious for the purpose of self-exploration, healing and creativity, Guided Imagery is more directive and is verbal; the guide often suggests the imagery. In the GIM method, the music does the suggesting. As the traveler talks about the images while the music plays, the guide makes comments or asks questions about the images for more in-depth exploration. Since the images are the traveler's own spontaneous creations, they are more in tune with the traveler's unconscious than any images the guide could invent. Travelers may find themselves somewhere as down-to-earth as a Hawaiian beach, or in a place as other-wordly as an outpost on Mars. The guide may ask, "What is it like there?" "Are you alone?" "How do you feel in this place?"

In an altered state of consciousness, the GIM traveler feels safe to let the music help him experience feelings that have previously seemed extremely threatening. The guide makes notes and, when the music ends, both the traveler and guide reflect upon the session together. With the guide's non-judgmental support, the traveler often finds the courage to confront current life issues or long-buried trauma and begin to deal with them. The music provides the supportive and loving channel for expression. The first step may be to acknowledge that these feelings exist. As Marion Woodman has observed:

> *Most people are operating on the persona, which is the showpiece, the masquerade. They are performing–they aren't in touch with their real feelings, and in a given situation they don't know if they're angry or if they want to cry. They are unhappy about not being able to express their emotions and also terrified to do so, because expressing them has led to rejection.*[2]

A woman in her forties who had been depressed for years came to me for a series of GIM sessions. Her life simply wasn't working, and she had no idea why she was blocked. In her second GIM session, as she listened to the music, she saw elegant musicians performing the music. However, when she went behind the scenes, she discovered unmade beds, clothes hanging out of drawers, and dust balls everywhere. She said it was like "uncovering secrets not known to the general public; that appearances weren't everything, and that everyone has a dirty closet." Here the traveler acknowledged her own mask, her own deception.

In a subsequent session, she saw herself sitting next to a giant onion, peeling away the layers of protective coating. Very soon she realized that the onion represented herself, and although the layers served a purpose (they protected her from hurt and pain), they had hardened into a brittle shell. She felt the shell both protecting and isolating her. The color of the shell was "intellectual gray." She felt a need to break the shell.

The GIM tape she was listening to was not only instrumental but had a choral section. The choral voices often feel very supportive, as though they are communicating strength to the imager. This woman felt as though the voices were giving her the courage to break the shell. She imagined that the voices were singing, "We're here for you; we're with you all the way." With the support of the music, she was able to break the shell that kept her from relationships with others.

During another GIM session, a woman in her late thirties who worked as a manicurist but was also a professional singer, was weighed down by feelings of helplessness in her life. The sound of the harp on the GIM Relationships tape became a metaphor to her for letting go and allowing a higher power to direct her life. After the session, she wrote this poem:

> *I am a harp*
> *Every string of which*
> *Resonates in the universe*
> *When I allow myself*
> *To be plucked*
> *By the Divine Harpist.*
>
> *I am nothing*
> *Without the hand of the Musician;*
> *And when the music leaves my strings,*
> *Only an instrument remains.*

A year later, after 12 GIM sessions, she wrote:

> *It is really difficult to put into words that which has become part of my innermost nature. Guided Imagery and Music has been a passage toward wholeness in my life which has enabled me to see life in living, brilliant color instead of black and white. There is only one Source of Universal Energy and I have learned how to let that flow into me so it can flow back out; sort of like getting a Heavenly jump start to recharge one's Earthly batteries!*
>
> *I do not try to fix the whole world anymore, but nurture that which is*

already whole and beautiful in others. Of course this human life is a process, and I do not presume to think that through GIM or any other means, I have "arrived." I hope to keep GIM as an energizing, nurturing, growing part of my life on an ongoing basis.

Guided Imagery and Music has empowered me to use the gifts that have been given to me, with love, and without embarrassment.

Many of us would rather go through life suffering guilt, free-floating anxiety, deep depression or a perennial state of joylessness than experience—even for a moment—unpleasant, painful emotions. Yet if we stuff these bad feelings down deep into our minds and bodies,they become sores that fester inside us.

We are taught at an early age that it is wrong to show negative emotion, especially anger. Very few of us know how to express anger because it feels so frightening. Often, these feelings are imaged as a poison or infection of some kind. A 55-year-old woman had been carrying her anger and fear inside her all her life:

I see a ball of fire. Like a knot, or cramp. It looks like a clenched fist. I'm afraid to let go. The center of it is like a boil. I see it as an infection. Fear, anger, depression—they're all tied in. The boil is trying to dissolve. I feel the unclenching around my face and neck. (Tears begin to flow). It's dark. Dark and still. It's restful now. Fingers massaging my shoulder muscles. The fingers changed into music. The music is massaging it now. I'm impatient. I'd like to grab the spot and throw it away. I can't get to it. It's stuck there. 'Out, damned spot!' The music is saying, 'Out, out, out!' to me. Feels more like a release now. I have always hated anger. Being in a situation where anger was displayed has always bothered me. Anger is connected with hate. When someone's angry, it says, 'I hate you.'

As anger becomes an acceptable emotion, and this woman learns to release it as it comes up, she will probably get rid of her red hot mental boil. When guilt, anger and fear rise up to the surface with music, they can be expressed in drawing or creative writing. In this way, destructive impulses may be channelled into creative energies that will hurt neither the imager nor those around them. Once negative emotions are expressed with the aid of music, there is a release that opens the traveler to a sense of aliveness, bringing a new capacity for feeling.

Bringing Back Beauty

As much as we need to experience the bad feelings, there is a deep-seated need in our time to feel the beautiful feelings as well. Living in a mechanized world, we have forgotten how to resonate with beauty. Rather than experience and feel the beautiful things in our environment, we tend to analyze them, take them apart, and focus only on the details. I had the experience of total resonance with a piece of art when I first stood in a little museum in Florence and looked at Michaelangelo's statue of David. It was as though I were one with this magnificent sculpture. I understood its essence through my feelings. Modern life provides us with all too few of these peak experiences, and it takes some deliberate effort on our part to restore them to their rightful place.

Another way to bring beauty back into our lives is by spending more quiet time with nature. Not long ago, I was sitting on a rock in the Cascade Mountains of Washington state. I sat quietly, feeling the sun on my face, watching the flow of the mountain stream only a few feet in front of me. As I listened to the sound of that stream, I could feel its rhythm connecting with my own internal rhythms. I could feel my own aliveness. I could feel the music of the Cosmos playing within me.

Many of us have lost our relationship with the natural universe; with those parts of life that are vibrant and growing. Listening to music can help us feel that connection again. If you have only five or ten minutes and you can't physically reach a meadow or a lake, let music take you there. Let it take you to a place where you can feel still, where you are no longer a slave to your own controlling tendencies, to your own stubborn insistence on directing where your mind goes. Let the music show you soft, green, fragrant grass; feel it under your bare feet. Let it seduce you with the rippling melody of the clear stream; cup your hand and taste its cool freshness. Drape yourself languidly over a sun-warmed rock, and feel its weathered, eternal texture. Take in the natural beauty with all your senses. Time will seem to slow down. You will begin to feel great joy or quiet serenity. It is a joy very different from the "high" experienced at a Saturday football game. It is stronger and more intense.

These poems were written at a workshop in fifteen minutes after listening to Debussy's Sacred and Profane Dances. They were spontaneous responses to the music:

Come, come, please dance with me.
Up the hill and down again.
And then, oh let us soar away
Where no gravity can pull us down.

Maidens let your long hair flow
And let your soft, slender arms
Undulate to the tone of the spheres.
And men bounce on while bubbling clouds
Rejoice, rejoice.

> *Oh to be back in Shepherd's meadow. The snow is so white and clean. It feels good to swish along across the middle. Should I write my name? Stretching my stride in a diagonal still feels so great. Tired of being cooped up inside! The sky is so blue, always so clear and sharp. The wind has just enough rip to rosy up my cheeks but not enough to make a hat a dire need.*
>
> *Warming the air as it comes into my body feels good; I like the contrast. One more loop through the meadow. You think you can beat me through the trees? We'll see. I've been through those twists, turns and twining stuff more times than you have! Watch that turn, here we go! The frost looks so pretty on the pine needles, in this lace pattern. Let's head back.*

As we create these altered states within our minds, the pleasure they bring our bodies and hearts is a source of relaxation and healing. Because your own unique imagination has taken you there, the natural universe you have imagined will infuse your being with harmony—a harmony only you can create. You have begun listening to the music of your deeper self.

Music Activity #3:
Deep Listening

Dr. Helen Bonny, developer of GIM, discovered that it is possible to connect with your deep feelings through music if your body is relaxed and your mind is focused. This exercise uses music to draw up from the unconscious images and symbols that may represent people or situations in your life. These images may provide you with insight into how you are really feeling and experiencing these situations. They may help you to re-experience repressed feelings, both sad and joyful.

Don't be concerned if you don't have a Technicolor motion picture playing in your mind. Many people find it difficult to visualize, yet are able to have powerful experiences with the music through their other senses. Bodily or kinesthetic response can be even more effective for connecting with emotions than a visual response.

If you don't feel as though you have to visualize your images, and you understand that "feeling images" or kinesthetic images are okay, you will find that visual images will suddenly begin to pop up out of nowhere. People who do not visualize easily find it happens naturally with music as a catalyst.

When I first began Music Imaging, I did not see any visual images. I was told it was all right to make them up because what I was making up was still coming from my own consciousness. I let go to the process. All of a sudden, a big, furry koala bear showed up. I had no idea where he came from! He turned out to be an image guide for me who often came into my imagery and enabled me to heal my old wounds.

Don't worry about your drawing ability either. You don't have to be a Leonardo: stick figures or abstract designs are just fine. It doesn't have to look exactly right to be a valid representation of your imagery.

As a musical accompaniment to this exercise, you can use the *Pachelbel Canon in D.*

Have your journal or sketch pad close by, go to your quiet place, relax, and get ready to begin.

○ Relax your body by doing some simple stretching or progressive relaxation (tensing and relaxing the muscles of your body, from your toes to your head).

○ To focus your mind, bring to your imagination a nature scene: a meadow, the seashore, a waterfall or a favorite place, and explore it. Using all your senses, notice what the place looks like, whether the air feels warm or cool, if there are sounds you might hear in this place or any fragrances you can smell. If you prefer, instead of a scene in nature you may choose to explore natural objects, such as a flower, a seashell or a gemstone.

○ Turn on the music

○ As you listen to the music, allow your mind to drift. Invite the music to bring you images, colors, shapes, fragrances, feelings of joy or sadness, memories.

○ Let yourself go wherever your imagination takes you. Don't place any restrictions on what you think about or feel, even if it seems strange or unexpected. Follow any paths that arise in your imagination, and take them as far as you would like to.

○ When the music has ended, gently bring your imagery to a close and bring yourself back to your room.

○ Take your sketch pad and draw the impressions that came up with the music. Notice, in particular, any deep feelings you might have connected with. Afterwards, you may want to write about these feelings in your journal, as follows:

Date:

Musical Selection:

Impressions:

Associated Memories and Feelings:

What can I do to honor this experience and make it work for me? For example, in the case of the koala bear, I bought the biggest, furriest stuffed koala bear I could find and kept it in my room.

Try this activity with other pieces of music. Try it again with the same piece of music on another occasion and see if the music elicits different responses. After doing this activity regularly, notice if you are more in touch with your feelings, and are able to express them more easily and openly. Notice how the release of sad or angry feelings affects the way you function at home or at work. Be aware of the joyful feelings, as well, allowing them to permeate everything you do. Watch your "frozen feelings" melt, and jot down in your journal the changes you note in:

o Your relationships

o Healing of old wounds

o Productivity at work

o Creativity level

o Ability to concentrate

o Ability to relax

o Energy level

o Health

If you can share this activity with another person, it will be doubly effective because you will be validating your imagination. When you talk about your imagery with someone else, it becomes more real since it then enters the physical universe. Also, when you exchange your imagery with another person, you open your mind to the fact that what you image may not be what another person may image, and yet they both have value. It helps make your thinking less rigid and expands your sense of connection with others.

Music Activity #4
Handling Negative Emotions

Here is another activity you might try. Read *Hoby Hyfop,* the story that follows. *Hoby Hyfop* is the first of four metaphorical stories included in this book. The language used is designed to stimulate all the senses and reach the unconscious. You may enjoy these stories in several ways:

1. You may read the story silently or aloud.

2. You may read the story to the *Mendelssohn Symphony No. 4, "Italian."*

3. A tape of the story read to music is available (See order form in the back of this book). Music, story and voice are orchestrated to evoke a powerful response from the unconscious. Listen in a relaxed position with your eyes closed, noticing the feelings and images that come up.

Hoby Hyfop, a creature from another planet, refuses to deal with his anger and frustration, which he thinks of as "being attacked by the raving rizzles." He learns that suppressing them doesn't work, and he learns to express them and let them go. While you read this story and imagine the situations in it, notice which parts of your body become tense and which ones stay relaxed. Notice what sort of physical and emotional reactions you have to the words and ideas.

This story is one you might find particularly rewarding to share with your own child. Discussing the story, making notes and drawing whatever *Hoby Hyfop* brings to mind, may help both of you come to terms with your unexpressed angers.

Hoby Hyfop

Once, on a planet somewhat like earth, called Hyfopia, there lived some highly intelligent creatures who were known as hyfops. Though at times they felt human, they were actually made of rubber, so that instead of walking, they simply bounced around. They came in all sizes and shapes, but there was one thing they all had in common. They could stretch themselves in different directions. Some days they would wake up and feel themselves stretching upward, while other days they stretched outward. When they went to sleep at night they never knew which way they would be stretching the next morning. Even their hearts were rubbery, and they could feel things bouncing up and down and all around deep inside them.

One of the most flexible of these creatures was called Hoby. Hoby always won all the games on the planet because he was so good at stretching. He could catch a ball from very far away simply by stretching out his arm, sometimes as far as 25 feet, until he could reach it. All the hyfops on the planet thought he was wonderful. In fact, they thought he was perfect.

But Hoby knew he was not. He had a problem he had never told anyone about. His problem was the raving rizzles, those nasty flying creatures who would come out of nowhere whenever something bad happened to him. Whenever he quarreled with a friend, or did poorly on a test at school, or sometimes for no reason he could figure out, the rizzles would descend on him. They would start rzzing and rzzing around his head in circles, making him dizzy. Lately, they had been attacking more frequently, and the battles had become more violent. Each time they struck, he felt like a piece of putty, unable to fight back. As if this weren't enough, Hoby had heard that the rizzles were capable of casting horrendous spells that could make a hyfop an alien being.

One day, Hoby was bouncing along feeling very high, when suddenly, two buoyant hyfops came rolling down the hill at great speed. They saw Hoby, changed direction, and deliberately knocked him down, rolled over him, and sped away, leaving Hoby lying flat on his back. Hoby was angry, but there were two of them, and only one of him, so he thought it was foolish to bounce after them. At that moment he felt like a balloon blowing itself up.

Then he heard a noise that sounded like rzzz, rzzz, rzzz, and he knew the raving rizzles were going to attack. A huge swarm of them were invading the hanging silence. They circled his head again and again in a rzzing crescendo that would not let up. Hoby plugged up his ears with his fingers, but still the sound was deafening. When it was at its ear-piercing loudest, the rizzles broke right through his vulnerable rubber skin. They swarmed around his chest, half of them on his left side, the other half on his right. Each half pulled and yanked as if he were a piece of taffy. His chest stretched and stretched like a rubber band, tightened, and would not snap back.

Then the rizzles flew into his lungs. They pushed his breath along in short staccato puffs while they rzzed to a rapid beat, convincing his heart to join them. It beat faster and faster until it bounced around from his head to his feet and could not find its proper place again. Then they grabbed his shoulders, pulled them up and placed them right under his ear.

They swarmed up to his face. They squeezed it and scrunched it into a tiny, hard ball. His eyes had become little slits and he could hardly see. They tied his two rubber legs together in a great big knot so he could not move. Hoby Hyfop felt humiliated until he realized he still had strength in his stretchy arms and hands. He reached out and expanded his hand until it was as large as a parachute. He caught all the rizzles in his hand and closed his fist. He could hear them rzzing helplessly beneath his fingers. Hoby had no idea how to get rid of them. Then, he thought: why not just put them in his bottom dresser drawer? And that is what he did. From then on, whenever Hoby felt angry or frustrated and the rizzles attacked him, he grabbed them quickly and stuffed them in his bottom drawer.

Soon, every one of his dresser drawers was filled with rizzles. Whenever he came into his bedroom, they would rzzz and bzzz angrily at him. Oddly enough, however, only he was able to hear them. Although his mother was often in his room, she seemed unaware of the loud insect humming that Hoby could hear quite clearly from his dresser drawers.

By now, Hoby had stopped putting his clothes and toys into it. They were heaped in piles on his bed, on the table, and scattered around the floor. His mother became very angry with him.

"You've always been pretty neat," she said to him. "What's gotten into you, Hoby?" But Hoby could only tell her that he had begun to dislike his dresser very, very much.

So Hoby's mother brought him a new chest of drawers and had the old one put in the basement. The rizzles didn't like that at all. It was dark and damp in the basement, and they couldn't upset Hoby by rzzing loudly because he never, ever went down to the basement. Something had to be done! They decided to cast a spell on Hoby.

In each drawer they swarmed, rzzing and bzzing. The dresser almost burst with the furious activity of their rapidly beating wings. The smell of rizzle fury—a gaseous substance that resembled resin—floated out through all the cracks in the dresser and in no time at all reached Hoby's nostrils.

At that moment, Hoby was in the middle of a ball game. Suddenly, Hoby felt his whole body stiffen up. His legs could no longer bounce around. His arms had no stretch to them at all. He could not imagine what was happening to him. He tried to bounce home, but all he could do was clunk about, one foot after the other, like a wind-up toy.

When he got home, he shut the door of his room behind him and took a good look at himself in the mirror. What had happened to his resilient hyfop self? Instead of flexible legs and pliable arms, his limbs were made of wood; all of him was hard, rigid wood, even his face. He wanted to cry, but wooden creatures cannot cry. He knew, of course, that it was the rizzles.

He went down to the basement. In the half light, he could see the dresser shaking with the combined fury of the thousand, thousand rizzles that were imprisoned inside it.

Hoby was terrified. What would happen if he let them loose? Would they rizzle him into insensibility? But he knew that nothing could be worse than the way he felt right now. Or rather, the way he could no longer feel. He had to take the chance.

He clunked over to the dresser and swiftly opened all the drawers. The thousands of rizzles flew out in an explosion of energy. They swarmed around Hoby's head and body for a few moments, holding him in a cylinder of rzzing, bzzing rizzles.

Hoby stood very still and tried to make them understand that he had imprisoned them because he was afraid of them; that he knew now that it was better to let the rizzles come when they had to, that feeling bad or angry or frustrated was better than trying to never feel anything at all.

With a tremendous explosion that was so loud it cracked the basement window, the rizzles turned, and as one being, flew out toward the sunlight. The noise also cracked Hoby's body of wood, revealing his old familiar rubberyness. Oh, how good it was to be able to stretch! Hoby stretched until his head hit the basement ceiling. He stretched his arms until the right one was at the window and the left all the way at the top of the stairs, holding the doorknob that opened into the kitchen. How wonderful it was to be a Hyfop again!

From that day on, Hoby Hyfop has never feared the raving rizzles, for every once in a while he needs them to remind him he is not a creature of wood, but a flexible, living, bouncing inhabitant of the planet of Hyfopia.

♪ ♪ ♪

Now that you've listened to the story of *Hoby Hyfop,* jot down your reactions to it.

o Was there a difference in the way you perceived the story when you first read it to yourself and then when you read it or heard it read aloud with music?

o When the raving rizzles swooped down on Hoby Hyfop, did your pulse rate speed up, your muscles tighten, or your breathing accelerate?

o How did you respond emotionally?

o Did the story/music remind you of similar situations in your own life?

o What can you do to get back in touch with your feelings?

Here is a learning experience for your body. Be Hoby Hyfop. Imagine you have turned to wood. Walk around the room as if you are wooden. Notice the rigidity in your body. Notice how heavily your arms and legs move. Now be Hoby Hyfop as a bouncing rubber being. Stand up and reach for the sky, and imagine your arms can reach three times as high as they actually can. Lie on the floor and lift your legs up as far as they can go, one at a time, and then stretch, stretch, stretch, as far as you can. Bounce around the room as if you are made of rubber. You are Hoby Hyfop!

If you have a child in the house, both of you acting out Hoby can be a shared, fun experience. If you are a teacher, you can have an entire class of Hoby Hyfops.

Notes

1. Leonard, George, *The Silent Pulse* (New York: Bantam Books, 1981), p.22–23.

2. Woodman, Marion, "Worshipping Illusions," *Parabola,* Vol XII, No. 2, May 1987, p. 62.

Three

Learning Can Heal

It is stress and tension that prevent learning.

—Dr. Georgi Lozanov

Children come to school with natural abilities, a wealth of knowledge and experience, and a sense of trust and openness that allows them, in the beginning, to absorb vast amounts of information on many levels. They are poets and painters, inventors and storytellers. They are not afraid to express themselves. For these children, living, breathing education thrives both outside of the classroom–in the world of experience—and inside their minds—in the world of imagination. The process of education as it is now designed, however, often tramples on their spontaneity, stamping it out before it has a chance to build on itself. All too often the classroom becomes a wasteland.

Author Joseph Chilton Pearce believes that child development has been truncated and retarded by an educational system that ignores the inner realm of imagery, intuition, and spontaneity, and pushes children into the more restricted realm of abstract reasoning before they are ready. Pearce sees schooling as a violation of self:

> *All that my early schooling did was to teach me to hate schooling, for we hate anything that thwarts our development, which is the basis for survival.*[1]

Children are not emotionless machines. They do not digest input like fact-swallowing computers. The way they process information is greatly influenced by their unconscious, emotional and intuitive promptings. If these more human aspects of learning are ignored, children often turn off and tune out. Many do poorly in school because they are forced to learn by rote. Our culture tends to see the purpose of education as simply to impart instruction, and the role of the teacher, to feed children facts.

But children cannot simply swallow facts whole. Their bright, whole brains want to connect these facts with other ideas or experiences. They need to understand how the facts relate to their own lives and how they can use them. Without this connection, they find the instruction vapid, meaningless and easily forgotten.

The failure of education to meet the needs of our students is reflected in a report from the Wall Street Journal which revealed that 700,000 high school students drop out of school each year. Students are simply not prepared to qualify for even the most menial jobs in business and industry. For example, 44 percent of the job applicants in a New Jersey office of Prudential Insurance Company could not read at the ninth grade level. Claiming that the U.S. "education factory" is obsolete, the Journal confirmed that the system has failed, and that we can't fix it by patching it up.[2] The continuing crisis in education today demands a reexamination of how people learn and how they are best taught. What we are doing is not working.

High school students interviewed recently by NBC television said they would rather be anywhere but in school. They feel imprisoned and bored. Most teachers will agree that problems that arise in the classroom stem, for the most part, from conflicts within individual students or from contention between individual students who find it difficult to relate to others. These conflicts often block learning and creativity, and result in students being labeled incompetent as a result of low scores on standardized tests. Rather than focusing on the healthful development of the whole person, school administrators, disturbed by these low test scores, choose to clamp down on both students and teachers, demanding higher quality work and more strict discipline. Because there is so little excitement in the classroom, students create their own excitement with disruptive behavior, while the teacher attempts to fill up what he considers the void between their ears.

But is there really a void? Our school systems are often programmed to focus on the result rather than the process of learning. We prize perfection over expression. Despite the fact that human beings were never designed to be perfect, but to *become*, both children and adults are constantly frustrated by being less than perfect people. Teachers and parents are often driven by the hidden hope that, since they themselves never attained perfection, perhaps their students or children will. Consciously or subconsciously, our children pick up that relentless push for perfection. Since they rarely experience being perfect, they are unable to accept themselves, or even like themselves. The resulting frustration may cripple their development.

In some cases, it has even led to teenage suicide, one of the gravest problems we face today. A study by the National Center of Health shows that every 78 seconds an adolescent attempts suicide. There is more and more evidence emerging that school experiences negatively influence a child's self-esteem. Another study revealed that, when they first enter school, 80 percent of children feel good about themselves. By fifth grade, only 20 percent have a positive self-image. By the time they graduate from high school, only 5 percent of seniors have good feelings about themselves. The cause of this drop in self-esteem is attributed to the proliferation of negative statements hurled at students over their twelve years of schooling, statements that reflect our expectations of perfection. Fortunately, many school districts are now beginning to form task forces to explore how education could foster self-esteem instead of crippling it.[3]

Perfection vs. Expression

Small children function mostly through unconscious processes. By the second grade, most children have begun to distrust their natural spontaneity. Their ability to reason, which is just developing, becomes overwhelmed by fears, worries, and anxieties. These negative emotions become enmeshed in their learning process and affect their learning capacity more than any of us can imagine.

If, rather than focusing on what they do wrong, a positive, joyful home and classroom ambience could be created where fears and anxieties were allayed, children would feel safe enough to express their unique feelings and ideas. More than A's and gold stars and "Excellents," our children need our support and encouragement to simply be themselves. They need our okay to show that Self to the world: to scribble it, dance it with their own made-up steps or sing it out, even if it's a little off-key.

Time and again, when I have visited elementary school classrooms in connection with my consulting work, I have come face to face with children's learned obsession with perfection. In one third grade classroom, I played a short piece of music, provided the students with brightly colored crayons, and asked them to draw the images that arose. Instead of reaching for the crayons and applying the colors, they started to draw with their pencils, erasing every line that wasn't perfect. They took out their rulers. Their main concern seemed to be with getting each line exactly right.

I suggested they use their crayons, choosing those colors they had seen in their imagery, and letting the images just flow. Perfection or artistic excellence didn't matter; they were to simply take the feelings and visual images from their imaginations and put them on the paper.

Many children found this very difficult to do. They were unable to function the way they were naturally designed to function; through the spontaneous and intuitive processes of their right brains. These young children were already being ruled by the ruler. They had lost their trust in their own natural capacity and had begun to believe that learning, even a right-brained activity like art, has to be painful, tedious and heavy with effort.

Some months later, I visited one of those classrooms again. At the end of the day, I asked the students what they had liked best about the day's activity. The answer: that I didn't care what the art work looked like. The important thing was they could just enjoy putting on paper whatever images came into their minds.

As parents and teachers, we have learned to value control, structure and discipline above all. We think that if learning is fun and effortless, the children are not really learning. But what is it our children need to learn?

There is no doubt that students must learn the technological languages of computers and other machines; those are useful and time-saving tools in today's world. But, as large corporations are beginning to discover, machines are fostering our isolation from ourselves and from each other. Worst of all, we have lost touch with our own humanness.

Our focus, as educators and parents, should be on helping our children to discover who they are deep inside. We can assist them to develop that unique Self. We can use their own self-knowledge and self-respect to foster a deeper understanding of others, and a greater respect for diverse ways of thinking and being.

Educators are beginning to realize that teaching creativity, self-esteem, peace, and social skills as part of the curriculum can revolutionize students' motivation and achievement levels. All of these skills are implicit in the accelerated learning format, so that learning becomes a deep, memorable, and integrative experience. A college president commented that aside from needing education that teaches basic skills, stresses problem solving, and helps them get jobs, students "need education which emphasizes our common humanity and which is concerned with our common problems and the ways that we together can solve them."[4]

Music, as a connector of hearts and minds, can help them do that. At the same time, as a vehicle for self-expression, music can help them appreciate their own unique contribution to the planet.

How Parents Can Help Their Children

Are you a perfectionist? If you grew up feeling the pressure to produce and "measure up," chances are you are imposing this value on your child. If that pressure is keeping your own Self in bondage, then you are probably transmitting that to your child subconsciously. Free yourself of your own inner nagging, and your child will begin to experience that freedom as well.

Doing music imaging activities with your child helps you experience your own expressiveness without judging it. It helps the child understand that there is not just one right way—the perfect way—to think or do something; that what we image when we hear a piece of music can be quite different from someone else's imaging, and yet be just as valid. It teaches children that our images are simply an expression of our uniqueness.

Through this activity your child may, perhaps for the first time, share with you his or her own fantasy visions. It will only take a few of these Music Imaging sessions to help her understand that whatever is inside is all right; that it is safe to let it out and express it through words, movement and art, even though it may not look beautiful or be perfect.

The following is an example of a child's first experiences with imaging to music. Notice the series of disjointed images. The child's imagination is being stimulated by the music and she is getting in touch with memories as well:

> *At the starting of the music it was exciting, like a person painting with long*
> *fast strokes, also a fountain with water springing up out of it, palm trees*
> *blowing in the breeze, a kitten playing with a ball of yarn making more of a*
> *tangle, more and more, a horse running on the beach, struggling to get out*
> *of water. The painter came back into the music. This song is like the first*

*time I learned how to skip in Ballet class. This part is where I fall down.
Dancing more and more, my sister climbing under the bed and getting
scratched by a cat. It was our old cat. A rope or Rapunzel's hair going down
to the prince. He's climbing up. Tries to escape with her from the evil witch.
My tooth is gonna come out.*

How Teachers Can Help Their Students

Actual instruction comprises only one-third of the learning process.
According to Dr Georgi Lozanov, pioneer in stress-free accelerated learning, learning consists of three parts: memory and intellect, education, and
health.

Lozanov's revolutionary work in education revealed that educators
need to pay more attention to students' mental and emotional health.
His research showed that school itself is a prime cause of stress:

> *Today, it is more clear than ever that there is a need to speed up and
> improve the methods of instruction and education without any additional
> burdening of the nervous system and without any harmful effects.*[5]

Lozanov pointed out that the incidence of neuroses, fatigue, and
other illness had become rampant in schools all over the world. He
defined "didactogeny" as illness or suppression of the development of
children due to the teacher's tactless approach.

Lozanov created a new approach to teaching and learning, which he
called Suggestopedia, since it is based on the science of suggestion. He
suggested that tapping what he calls "the reserve capacity of the brain"—
the 96% or so that we normally do not use—involves not only the assimi-
lation of the material taught, but healthy development of the personality,
and physical health and well-being. The therapeutic effects of music combined with art, drama, and relaxed concentration activate the unlimited
capacities of the "paraconscious," that is, all levels of the psyche that are
not conscious. This method, often called Accelerated Learning, involves
creating an environment of profound psychological understanding that
seeks to liberate and stimulate the personality, starting in early childhood.

Reporting the results of his research on the healthful effects of his educational system, Lozanov cites an experiment done in sixteen Bulgarian schools:

> *In the course of two years (1975-6 and 1977-8), 2,300 first and second graders were examined by a commission of twelve psychotherapists and four university professors. It was established that in the suggestopedic schools, neurotic disorders in children have decreased by half compared with those in the control schools. At the same time, the schoolchildren have learned a material [sic] twice as much as that given to the children in the control schools, and they have achieved that without any homework and under the conditions of a shortened working week.* [6]

Lozanov strongly believes that the reductionist paradigm is obsolete. He believes that an educational premise based on memorizing facts that are isolated from our practical experience is bound to fail, for it ignores the fact that *we are taught and educated by the environment and for the environment in which we live.*

Yet despite all that has been discovered in recent years about how the brain functions, and the unconscious, intuitive and emotional factors that influence learning, teachers are still focusing on facts. Often, this is through no fault of their own, as they are pressured by school administrators to emphasize testing and grades—areas that are easily measurable. Achievement is king.

The push to go "back to basics" that many schools have adopted in the eighties—longer hours, time on task, and more control—has created more stress for children and teachers than ever before. How important are grades when so many children are suffering from severe emotional distress? Today, the incidence of emotionally disturbed children in schools has reached epidemic proportions. Yet many educators still operate as generals leading an army of wounded soldiers. I remember feeling shocked when, in one of my accelerated learning training seminars for teachers, one told us that her administrator had instructed teachers not to smile in their classrooms until after Christmas. A second teacher confirmed that her principal had given her the same instructions, so as not to "lose control" of her students. After I sat down and recovered, we discussed what a powerful affirmative suggestion a smile really is, and how it can help children to learn by breaking down barriers to learning and creating a safe, non-threatening environment.[7]

An alarming number of children these days are dealing with dysfunctional families, fear of nuclear war, isolation, and repressed angers and hostilities. They are not willing or able to process information unless it is intimately related to their own lives, and is presented in such a way as to engage them on an emotional level. Insecurities from lack of nurturing in the early years, and feelings of abandonment often become interwoven with incoming information as it is encoded in the brain.

Many children are in need of a therapeutic environment. If their home and family situation cannot provide this, and in fact exacerbates the problem, teachers can learn to organize and orchestrate the learning environment so that psychologically and physically it becomes a place of healing. They can learn to stimulate and activate emotional, intuitive mechanisms in the brain that will engender the necessary connections that make learning exciting and lasting. They can learn how to make the classroom a safe and healing place where children can feel comfortable enough to learn to know themselves, and open enough to learn to know others. Rather than encouraging children to swallow their feelings, the healing classroom educates them to explore and express their feelings. Aggresion and anger, when allowed to come to awareness, and to be worked through in the imagination, are less likely to cause disruptive behavior. At the same time, inner processes take place that strengthen the ego, enabling children to learn more effectively and interact with greater social skills. Music, with its great capacity for reaching non-verbal places inside us, can teach these lessons.

As children listen to music in a relaxed, receptive state of mind, it evokes negative emotions that may be blocking them, as well as positive emotions that long to be released. Then, when the children draw feelings and images that arise out of their deep unconscious, they have made their inner world concrete. Sharing their drawings with others validates their feelings and opens them up to free expression of their inner selves.

And What About Helping the Teachers?

Working with Music Imaging helps teachers, too. So much is required of them in the way of paperwork, meetings and interfering menial tasks that their anxiety and fatigue level is as high as the students'. The music I teach them to use in the classrooms for their students has gratifying effects on them.

Some time ago, I gave a class in accelerated learning at the University of San Diego. Five of the teachers in my class were employed at the same elementary school. They all began to incorporate music into their curricula, using it cautiously, as I had suggested, so as not to overdose on it. They used it for story-telling, for rest periods, for smooth transitions from one activity to the next, for stimulating creative writing, and for silent reading and math, in order to help children focus their minds and effortlessly move into a state of relaxed concentration.

They became so enthusiastic at the results that each week when they returned to work from my class they would teach their colleagues all they had learned the night before. The staff would gather in the school lounge in a spirit of contagious excitement. The accelerated learning strategies they tried brought new life into their classrooms.

The next year, I trained an entire staff of San Diego teachers to incorporate music into their classrooms. The results were truly amazing: in just a few months, there was a substantial shift in their students' attitudes. The classrooms changed from tense, rigid, dull places to pleasant, enjoyable environments. The teachers themselves felt changed, and behaved differently toward their students. They became more relaxed and seemed to lighten up. Many of them, who had never before experienced classical music, could feel it balancing their bodies and their emotions.

Using Music Imaging, some teachers are starting to awaken to their inner selves and attend to their personal process of development. They have begun to allow the trusting, playful inner child they once were out to play. Even if this happens just during a short Music Imaging session at a workshop, the images often stay with them. At one of these workshops, a very conservative elderly teacher wrote this piece to the *Brandenburg Concerto No. 5* (second movement):

> *I am a Gypsy woman. I walk alone—unbound and unfettered. Sometimes I walk in concert with others but I am alone and free. I can smell the wildness of things and I hear only the natural rumbling of the world. I like who I am. I do not care to be bound by convention or tastes. My space is my own and my life is here. My spirit can soar at my bidding and can reflect at its own time. I am free.*

The Healing Home/The Calm Classroom

Music can soothe, calm and heal. It can also bring joy—and joy is therapeutic. Calming music acts as a balancing, structuring influence; stimulating music, by breaking down emotional blocks, can also be therapeutic. Music can bring concord into discord. It can bring beauty into the ugliness of conflict and chaos.

Tracy, a fourth grader who lives in Watts, an inner city district of Los Angeles, has many learning problems. Usually one cannot make sense of what she writes. I was stunned by Tracy's composition, written after listening to the slow movement of the *Beethoven Symphony No. 6, "Pastoral"* (second movement):

> *I saw a beautiful land in the woods. The animals started coming out of the bushes, and the flowers were blooming. Butterflies were coming, and a bird was sitting on my finger. The bird was red and black. When I went home, I wished I was in a land like that.*

This experience, which many adults would consider useless fantasy and a waste of time, may be this child's only contact with beautiful feelings. Its therapeutic effect will be evident not only in her attitude and behavior but in her receptivity to learning. Letting in the birds will help her to fly.

Music should be used in the home as well as in the classroom for healing and therapeutic purposes. When children are feeling aggressive or hyperactive, music can calm them down, soften their aggression and help them let go of obsessive behaviors. Parents and teachers can play the music without drawing attention to it and notice if there are any changes in the children's behavior.

Even more effective is to set aside a little time, even just a few minutes, for a musical activity. After recess at school, or an outdoor play period at home, children may be asked to lie down or put their heads down on a desk or table. They then listen to three or four minutes of a calming piece of music such as the *Pachelbel Canon in D* (children of all ages love this piece of music), or the slow movement of a Vivaldi flute concerto. The sound of the flute soothes them, and the precise, structured beat makes them feel secure.

Dr. Alfred Tomatis, a French physician, believes that music energizes the brain, as well as relaxes it. Tomatis' early research led him to an abbey in France where, as a result of the elimination of their six to eight hours a day of Gregorian chanting, the monks had lost their energy. As soon as they resumed chanting, their high energy returned. Musician and educator Don Campbell trained teachers to apply aspects of Tomatis' work in several U.S. schools, and found it useful in awakening childrens' latent abilities.

The Moyers Center for Learning in San Diego now provides Tomatis programs for children and adults, to improve motivation, listening, communication and the ability to learn more effectively. Pat Moffitt Cook, Ph.Dc., M.M., Director of the Open Ear Center for Music and Healthcare, and Emila Flores, Tomatis listening therapist of the Dallas Listening Center, have helped launch this successful program. Parents report improved social skills and motor coordination for sports activities, enjoyment of school, and a sense of wellbeing.

For calming hyperactive children, Dr. Helen Bonny[8] recommends a light, sedative type of music, such as *Massenet's "Dimanche Soir"* from *Scenes Alsaciennes*. Hal Lingerman[9] recommends different types of music for hyperactive children depending on whether they are aggressive or more introspective types. The latter benefit most from Impressionistic music, such as Debussy or Respighi, whereas active children might begin with a march, followed by a Vivaldi or Telemann flute concerto.

Teachers and parents are often reluctant to experiment with classical music because they do not know enough about it. But a high school teacher who tried starting the school day with a few minutes of music found that her students were much more receptive to learning. She said:

> *My first period class, a class for those who have failed other English classes, is noted for having students whose home lives are chaotic, and whose behavior is disruptive. They're always being called down to the office for various infractions and, generally speaking, school and home are often not very pleasant places for them to be.*
>
> *After taking your class, I have experimented with having them come in and listen to some classical music, usually Mozart or Beethoven, because I am familiar with those composers, for about four or five minutes at the beginning of the period. I tell them that they may just listen to the music or daydream or whatever they wish. Sometimes I have them write afterwards, but not always.*
>
> *My primary objective has been to have them let go of whatever might be interfering with learning, and to make them more receptive to whatever we're doing in class. At first, the musical interlude was met with loud protests and complaining but, after about two or three days, most people really liked it and now they check to see if we can do this every day.*
>
> *To me, this is a great way to set the stage for whatever I'm going to do in class and, more importantly, to help my students put some distance between themselves and whatever is going on in their lives that might block their learning. As a bonus, it also does the same thing for me.*

There are no hard-and-fast rules about which music to use; there are only guidelines. Begin by trying some of the pieces recommended in this book, and then try others. You will be able to tell by your and your chil-

dren's reactions and responses what is appropriate. Use music that is harmonious and does not contain a great deal of dissonance and discordance.

On the children's tape of the Music Rx series, Dr. Bonny suggests
light, uplifting pieces of music such as *On the Trail* by Grofé from the
Grand Canyon Suite or *Flight of the Bumble Bee* by Rimsky-Korsakov. Dr.
Lozanov's recommendations of music that has been scientifically tested
and found to be beneficial to young children include the *Symphony No.
101, "The Clock,"* by Haydn and *Eine Kleine Nachtmusik* by Mozart.

Some of this music can also be used with teenagers, but they would
probably tend to relate better to the music recommended for adults. Be
sure to write down which pieces of music seem to be therapeutic for the
children, and also jot down your own responses. Then you will know
which pieces to use the next time your students tumble into class after a
fist fight on the playground, or your child comes hopping home and can't
seem to stop his hopping long enough to take a nap.

Music Activity #5
Imaging With Children

The purpose of this activity is to encourage your child to talk about
his or her feelings, fears, desires and needs.

o Each of you get comfortable

o Tense and relax your muscles together, talking your child through the
sequence from toes to head. Ask your child to imagine she or he is in
a favorite place outdoors and, at the same time, imagine that you are
in your favorite place. You might say something like this:

"Notice what you see around you in this place; what you see way
out in the distance and up close to you. Notice what the air feels like;
whether it's warm or cool. Notice what the ground feels like under
your feet. Let the music come into this scene with you and let it take
you wherever you want to go."

o Turn on *Prelude to the Afternoon of a Faun*. This piece is light and
impressionistic and evokes lots of imagery.

○ Emphasize again that you both can go wherever the music takes you, then let the piece play all the way through.

○ After the music has ended, each draw your impressions. Remember that this is not a test. There are no grades, just pleasure in expressing on paper the images that come up in your mind. There are no extra points for perfect execution.

○ Talk about what each of you has experienced. It is an avenue of expression for you both, without self-imposed judgment or criticism. Talk about your own drawing first. Discuss the feelings you had, so that your child can feel free to discuss his own feelings. Then make some interested comment about their drawing, such as "I'd love to know more about that colorful bird." This sort of comment is much more effective for bringing out their feelings than "What a beautiful picture" or "What's that in the corner?" Encourage your child to tell you as much as possible about the objects they have drawn and how she or he feels about them.

○ Put your drawings on the refrigerator or hang them up in your rooms.

Music Activity #6
Stimulating Imagination

The purpose of this activity is for you and your child to bring to the surface and share your innermost fantasies with each other.

○ Find a comfortable place to relax.

○ Take a few deep breaths.

○ Give your child a five minute back massage.

○ To help both of you focus your minds, ask your child to imagine the following, and do the same, yourself:

"Imagine your favorite animal. Notice how big it is and what it looks like. It can be any color you wish. Pretend that your animals.has wings and can fly. Notice what its wings look like. Reach out and touch them and notice what they feel like. Imagine that you can fly with your animal. Allow yourself to get on its back, and when the music comes on, let it take you and your animal wherever you want to go."

○ Turn on *Eine Kleine Nachtmusik*. Allow about 15-20 minutes long.

○ After the music is over, each of you write about your adventure.

○ Share your adventures with each other.

Music Activity #7
Balancing Children in the Classroom

Activity A: Focusing Attention

Children often come into school with negative emotions and distracted minds. This next technique helps them clear and focus their minds, enabling them to become more receptive to learning.

○ In the morning, when your students arrive, after you have made your announcements and gone through logistics, have the students put their heads down on their desks and close their eyes. Suggest that they listen to the music and let their imaginations follow the music wherever it leads them.

○ Play four minutes of *The Four Seasons*. If the students seem tired and unenergetic, even in the morning, try the first movement of "Spring." If they are hyper and distracted, use a slow movement.

○ Have students briefly share their imagery.

○ Use the fast movements of this piece to counteract afternoon burnout.

Activity B: Background Music

When children are doing any kind of silent desk work–art, math, reading, etc.–play one of the *Brandenburg Concertos*. Notice whether or not the students are able to concentrate better, do higher quality work, have less anxiety, or find the work more pleasant.

Activity C: Stimulating Emotions and Imagination

To stimulate students' imagination and emotions for creative writing classes, play *Eine Kleine Nachtmusik*. Take the following steps:

○ Have the students stand up and take some deep breaths. Then have them shake the kinks out of their bodies.

○ To focus their minds, choose one of the following:

If a definite topic is not assigned, suggest a nature scene or object.

If there is an assigned topic, ask the students to bring to mind an image that relates to the topic at hand. For example, if you wanted them to write about Christopher Columbus, you might say:

"Imagine that you could be sailing with Christopher Columbus on his ship. Notice what he looks like. What color are his eyes? What is the shape of his nose? What kind of a mouth does he have? What color is his hair? What sort of an expression does he have on his face? Notice what he's wearing, and what he has on his feet. See if he has anything to say to you. Let the music help you to imagine what your voyage together would be like."

○ Have the students close their eyes, put their heads down on their desks and listen to the music.

○ When the music is over, rewind the tape, play it again, and have the students write about their experience with the music. Ask for volunteers to come up to the front of the room and share their adventures.

○ Notice if the children:

⇨ Write more prolifically with music.

⇨ Write more imaginatively.

⇨ Listen to each other more intently and are more interested in each other's compositions.

⇨ Are using better grammatical structures.

⇨ Are more stimulated to discuss their compositions.

Activity D: Musical Self-Therapy for Teachers.

You can make teaching less stressful and tiring with the appropriate use of music. If you are aware of what pieces to use when, and their effect on you, you will find that you have more energy to give to your life outside school. As you play music during the day, notice its effect on you, as well as on the children. Notice how you react, and jot down your impressions in your journal. Try the following pieces to help support you during the challenges you face each day:

o Listen to the *Four Seasons* in the morning on your way to class to fill you with anticipation for the day.

o On days when you feel scattered and unfocused, try playing the Brandenburg Concertos.

o When you simply need a break from it all; some unstructured time—even if it is only a few minutes—allow your mind to wander with Eine Kleine Nachtmusik or with the Pachelbel *Canon in D*. Do you feel more relaxed after your mind has taken a vacation?

o When you feel your energy running low, renew yourself by listening to *The Four Seasons*.

o Do you find you have more energy *after* school since using music as a tool toward wholeness?

Here are the experiences of three teachers, commenting on teaching to music.

The first day I played music, I played Vivaldi's Four Seasons. I give all the children a daily timed math drill with 100 facts. The first group of children I worked with appeared to work faster and more efficiently. Several of the students well surpassed their previous scores. My aide and I were absolutely shocked, because many times, these students come into my classroom dragging their feet, dead tired from lack of sleep.

Relaxing and visualizing to the music is much more productive when I look at what I've accomplished compared to what I produce without the music, both in terms of quantity and quality. I notice the same thing with my students. When they listen to music and then write, they seem to have more ideas, more parts of themselves to put down on paper. The music, by freeing some of their creative energy, enables them to write and write and write.

While visualizing and listening to music, it is the sheer beauty of the music that sometimes overwhelms me, not in an analytical sense where I notice each part and instrument, but in a purely emotional way, where the music crashes over me and vibrates through me, and takes me with it. It is this sense of joy as I am learning or creating, or as my students are learning or creating, that really matters to me, and I think to myself, "This is what learning should be like." This laughing and happiness and sheer pleasure in the experience is what learning should be always, and if music is what can help bring this joy to my classroom, then I must not be without it.

Music Activity #8
Therapeutic Music for Children

The following lists of musical selections to use with children have been developed by me and others (where noted). They have been shown to have beneficial effects by experimentation and experience:

For Children *In Utero* and Infancy:

J.S. Bach	Flute Sonatas
Beethoven	Piano Concerto No. 5 (second movement)
Brahms	Lullaby
Humperdinck	"Children's Prayer," From *Hansel and Gretel*
Mozart	Concerto for Flute and Harp
	Violin Concerto No. 5 in A major
	Sinfonia Concertante
Vivaldi	*The Four Seasons*
	Flute Concertos
	Violin Concertos

For Hyperactive or Disturbed Children:

J.S Bach	Air on a G String
	Arioso from Cantata No. 156
	The Brandenburg Concertos
Brahms	Violin Concerto (second movement)
	Lullaby
Handel	*Water Music*
Haydn	Cello Concerto in C major (second movement)
Mendelssohn	*On Wings of Song*
Mozart	Concerto for Flute and Harp

Pachelbel	Canon in D
Vivaldi	*The Four Seasons*

Note: You might want to begin with *The Four Seasons* or *The Brandenburg Concertos* to match the high energy and help the children to focus, then move on to a slower, calmer piece of music.

For Repressed Children:

Any composer	Gregorian Chants
Beethoven	Symphony No. 6, "Pastoral"
Brahms	Piano Concertos 1 and 2
Copland	*Appalachian Spring*
Dukas	*The Sorcerers Apprentice*
Handel	*Royal Fireworks Music*
Haydn	*Toy* Symphony
	String Quartets
Mozart	Piano Concertos No. 21 and 23
	The Magic Flute
Prokofiev	*Peter and the Wolf*
Wagner	*Ride of the Valkyries*

For Young Children:[10]

Anderson	*Typewriter Symphony*
	Serenata
	Bugler's Holiday
	Syncopated Clock
Debussy	*La Petit Suite*, "Cortege," "Ballet"
Grainger	*Spoon River*
Grofé	*Grand Canyon Suite*
	On the Trail
	Mississippi Suite
	Huckleberry Finn
Kodaly	*Hary Janus*
	Viennese Musical Clock

Massenet	*Scenes Alsaciennes,* "Dimanche Soir"
Murooka, Hajime	*Lullaby From the Womb*
Paganini	*Moto Perpetuo*
Prokofiev	March from *Peter and the Wolf*
Rimsky–Korsakov	*Flight of the Bumble Bee*

For Elementary School Children:[11]

Beethoven	Romance No. 1 for Violin & Orchestra in G major
Handel	*Water Music*
Haydn	Symphony No. 82 in C major
	Symphony NO. 101 in D major, "The Clock"
Leopold Mozart	*Children's* Symphony
	Peasant's Wedding
	A Musical Trip with a Sled
Mozart	Violin Concerto No. 5 in A major
	Eine Kleine Nachtmusik
	Piano Concerto in F major
Tchaikovsky	Violin Concerto in D major
	The Four Seasons
	Twelve Pieces for Piano
Vivaldi	*The Four Seasons*

Additional Selections for Young Children:[12]

Bizet	*The Children's Games*
Chopin	Piano Concerto No. 1
Debussy	*The Children's Corner*
	Golliwog's Cakewalk
Mendelssohn	*On Wings of Song*
Ravel	*Mother Goose Suite,* The Empress of the Pagoda
	Mother Goose Suite, The Fairy Garden
Schumann	*Scenes from Childhood*
	"From Foreign Lands and Peoples"
	"A Curious Story"

| Schumann | *Traumerei* |
| Villa–Lobos | *The Family of Dolls* |

Notes

1. Pearce, Joseph Chilton, *Magical Child Matures* (New York: E.P. Dutton, Inc., 1985), p.2.

2. Graham, Ellen, "Retooling the Schools," *The Wall Street Journal,* March 31, 1989, p. R3.

3. *For Instructors Only,* Performance Learning Systems, 7/87, #9.

4. Levine, Arthur, *Newsletter of the Teacher Education Division,* Cal State Long Beach, April, 1985.

5. Lozanov, Georgi, *Suggestology and Outlines of Suggestopedy* (New York: Gordon & Breach, 1978), pp. 258-259.

6. *Ibid.,* p.226.

7. Merritt, Stephanie, *Successful, Non-Stressful Learning* (San Diego: Merritt Learning Systems, 1987), p.77.

8. From Music Rx tape series, *"Children's Tape,"* developed by Helen Bonny.

9. Lingerman, Hal, *The Healing Energies of Music* (Wheaton, Il.: The Theosophical Publishing House, 1983), p.69.

10. From *Music Rx, "Children's Tape,"* developed by Helen Bonny.

11. Lozanov, Georgi, *Suggestology & Outlines of Suggestopedia,* Gordon & Breach (New York), 1978, p. 234, 270. (Scientifically tested by Dr. Lozanov, using EEGs on the brain to determine which pieces of music lower brainwave frequency.)

12. Recommended by Karl Haas on his radio program, *Adventures in Good Music.*

Choosing Your Music

Music...must never offend the ear; it must please the hearer; in other words, it must never cease to be music.

—Wolfgang Amadeus Mozart

Classical Music

The question is inevitable: Why is classical music used primarily for learning, healing and self-exploration? Why not jazz, rock or other kinds of music?

The focus of this book is on classical music for two reasons: first, most music therapists and brain scientists who have studied the effect of music on the brain/mind agree that it has the greatest therapeutic value and potential for enhancing self-knowledge and self-development. Second, most parents and teachers have had very little exposure to classical music and know very little about it. Fortunately, we can educate ourselves about it by learning to listen to this music in a more conscious way and noticing its effect on our whole beings.

Classical music is a very powerful way to tap into greater sources of creativity. Most other kinds of music are simply not as effective. Rock, the dominant music of our age, cannot give the inspiration and spiritual connection most of us hunger for. These qualities cannot emerge from chaotic, disturbing sounds, since these sounds jar and disrupt the rhythms of our bodies and minds. You need to be in a centered, almost meditative state, with your physiological functions slowed down, in order to access your own deepest thoughts and insights.

In *The Secret Life of the Unborn Child*, Dr. Thomas Verny describes the effects of different kinds of music on the unborn fetus. He recounts experiments in which fetal distress was measured when different types of music were played. These experiments demonstrated that, even early in pregnancy, Vivaldi and Mozart are the unborn child's favorite composers. In one experiment, when their music was played,

> *...fetal heart rates invariably steadied and kicking declined. The music of Brahms and Beethoven, and all forms of rock, on the other hand, drove most fetuses to distraction. They kicked violently when records of these composers were played to their pregnant mothers.* [1]

To be most effective for releasing creativity, music must have tension and release. Dr. Lozanov pointed out that relaxation by itself is only a part of the process of activating the reserve capacities of our minds. The other part is concentration and motivation. What is it in the music that helps our minds to focus? Apart from physiological changes, such as the slowing down of the heart rate, breathing and brain waves, the harmony in classical music organizes the tones so that there is a sense of order and unity. When we listen, we feel that sense of order and it influences us subconsciously.

Of course, not every piece of classical music is ideal for every activity, and not all classical music is supposed to be soothing. I was once told by a young woman that she was having a great deal of difficulty studying to classical music; it was stimulating her and making her mind wander.

When I asked her what music she was using, she replied, "Beethoven's Seventh Symphony." That music, with its frequent changes and varied tone color, is more appropriate for emotional stimulation than for mental focus. On the other hand, a teenager I worked with became frustrated and upset with the *Beethoven Emperor Concerto* because it was "going all over the place." He was used to having his senses numbed by the loud, driving, heavily accented music he customarily listened to, music in which the percussion track is taped first and the melody then fitted in with the mechanical beat. *The Emperor Concerto* was piquing his imagination, prying open his feelings and affecting him on many levels at once. It was the positive emotional and mental stimulation he couldn't handle.

Obviously, not all classical music produces the same effect, and a little knowledge about the different periods of music and the varied effects they have on you will teach you how to use them to best advantage.

There is good music of all types. There is good jazz, enjoyed by many millions, but whose syncopation and irregular rhythms make it unsuitable for learning and therapeutic purposes. Some modern classical music, such as *Rite of Spring* by Stravinsky, may be very exciting to some listeners, but it is not considered therapeutic because of its discordant sounds. The Ravel Bolero, used in the movie "Ten," may be appropriate music for making love, but its insistent rhythms agitate emotions, and thus it would probably not inspire us to tap into deeper wisdom or creative genius.

Dr. Helen Bonny told me that she has found that Indian, Oriental or African music, although much of it is highly spiritual, is generally not as therapeutic for us as classical music, simply because ours is a Western culture and we are not accustomed to its sounds. On the other hand, Peter Hamel, in his book, *Through Music to the Self,*[2] finds that some Eastern and African music can awaken profound spiritual experiences for us as well as for those who grew up with them. Perhaps as divergent cultures begin to merge, a new universal music will evolve.

Other Western Music

The record and tape business is a multimillion dollar industry, and many composers are caught up in making music to make money. Bach wrote prolifically for the church, but money was not his primary objective. His major motivation for composing was to connect with the deeply spiritual sources within himself.

When we listen to the superficial, mechanical kind of music written by composers who have never transcended their own narrow, materialistic existences, we cannot learn much about harmonious relationships, our relation to the cosmos, and the transcendence of our own self-imposed limitations. This music reinforces our limited state, rather than challenging us to transcend those limits.

Dr. Lozanov claimed that certain classical music was written by "higher philosophical minds" that understood Eastern philosophies such as yoga, and that they wrote intuition and relaxation into their music. They were tuned into their deeper self that could draw inspiration from the Universal Mind.[3]

The core or essence of the composer is in his music. If he is a highly evolved, balanced human being, as Bach was, or if he has overcome huge tests and difficulties in his life, as Beethoven did, then his values, his strength, his victories and his integrity of character will be unconsciously understood and absorbed by those who listen to it, particularly if the performer is a clear channel through which the music may flow to the listener.

For instance, Beethoven's music, though stormy, is wonderfully uplifting. What we hear is a musical statement that no matter how difficult life is, we can somehow overcome our hardships. The music climbs higher and higher until it resolves in great triumph. Subconsciously, when we hear that music, we feel that victory.

New Age Music

New Age music is an emerging genre that has become quite popular, and is primarily used for relaxation and meditation. Its themes are often cosmic and global, environmental or ethnic. In general, it is simplistic in structure, often lacks direction or distinct melody lines, and sometimes has a spatial, open quality to it. Many people find this music relaxing and healing.

Many teachers are finding New Age music useful in the classroom for relaxing and clearing the mind in between the day's activities, much like a sherbet between the courses of a meal. Business executives also use it when their heads are swarming with facts and dates and they want to forget themselves for a while. (I myself find that a calming piece of Baroque music relaxes me even more and, at the same time, clarifies my thoughts, helps me focus, and puts me back into a state of balance and harmony.)

To discuss New Age music as a whole may be too broad a generalization, as hundreds of diverse pieces of contemporary music are now being categorized as "New Age." At the end of this chapter there is a list of selections that are suitable for relaxing or meditating. For an extensive array of good New Age music and the particular qualities of each selection, I recommend Hal A. Lingerman's book, *Life Streams*. Lingerman has spent hundreds of hours listening to New Age music and filtering out the tapes he finds most helpful.

To quantify the healing potential of New Age music, the Psychotronic Research Institute in California measured electromagnetic energy fields by using Kirlian photography and galvanic skin response, and found *Spectrum Suite* by Steven Halpern to be physically more relaxing than classical music. However, "The California researchers focused on relaxation without engaging the mind; they measured relaxation at the cellular and molecular levels of the body."[4] In contrast, Dr. Lozanov and Dr. Bonny use music that engages the imaginative, emotional, and intuitive aspects of the listener, as well as the physical. Halpern believes that the two approaches, classical and new age, are not mutually exclusive, and that both can be helpful in promoting relaxation, even though they do it in different ways.

I have made two important observations regarding New Age compared to Classical music for relaxation: (1) A deeper state of relaxation may be reached with the tension and release in classical music; after the tension, the sense of release is much greater, as in progressive relaxation exercises. (2) Some workshop participants and students in classrooms become irritable or get headaches from some of the new age music I have played.

So choose carefully. Many pieces of New Age music are mediocre at best and non-therapeutic at worst. Much New Age music meets Dr. Lozanov's first criterion: relaxation, but not the second: motivation. It lacks the structure to help us focus our minds and motivate us. Because of its limited scope of feeling, it might not reach as deep into our psyches as classical music with its tension and release, or evoke as wide a range of images. The lack of tension or forward movement may explain why many listeners do not feel inspired or deeply moved with most New Age compositions. As cosmic as they sound, they may not strike our spiritual chords in as life-changing a way as classical music does.

Author Joel Funk believes that in their effort to transcend ordinary consciousness, New Age music composers bypass the spiritual struggle so evident in the music of classical composers such as Beethoven. It is the struggle itself that makes transcendence so triumphant, and gives it support and groundedness. Even Mozart's music, often considered sweet and serene, contains some tension and release.

For learning and memory retention, and after experimenting with many different kinds of music, Dr. Lozanov chose classical music for his foreign language model. He tested hundreds of pieces of music using electroencephalograms (EEG's) of the brain to determine which pieces were most effective for reducing brain wave frequency. Then he tried out the pieces in foreign language classrooms.

As students listened to as many as 550 new words of a foreign language read by a trained teacher, Lozanov monitored their pulse and blood pressure, reliable indicators of stress. He found that despite the large volume of material students were given, rather than becoming stressed and anxious, their pulse rates actually slowed down, and in many cases their blood pressure was reduced.

The thrust of these experiments is clear: learning, when it is joyful and relaxed, is medicine that is easy to swallow! When American teachers began experimenting with other genres of music, such as popular or New Age music, Lozanov urged them to test its physiological effects before assuming their choices would yield the same results as the music he had chosen.

The music used on the GIM tapes has gone through similar rigorous selection and sequencing by Dr. Bonny, to demonstrate its ability to access unconscious resources. Although the body needs to be in a relaxed state, the purpose of GIM is not relaxation, and music which is designed solely for that purpose lacks the dynamics that can break through emotional blocks and melt frozen feelings.

The music I suggest in this book is thus probably most effective for our purposes here. However, this doesn't mean that you can't experiment with other selections for both learning and self-exploration. Certain New Age selections use unusual instruments and sounds, and I enjoy them very much when I'm in the mood for them. One that I particularly enjoy consists of mostly environmental sounds. It is called Machu Picchu Impressions, and when I listen to it, my senses are filled with the mysticism of the mountains of Peru.

How can you test the effect different pieces of music have on you? It is unlikely that you own an EEG or biofeedback machine, but you can measure your pulse rate and respiration, and notice other changes in your body. You can observe the impact of the music on your emotions, mental agility and spiritual nature.

Is Hard Rock Really Harmful?

Many rock fans who grew up on rock music in the sixties take offense at the lumping together of all rock music and calling it negative music. But certain kinds of rock have been found by a number of scientists to be harmful to the body, brain, emotions and soul. There are other kinds of rock, like the Beatles' music, and songs by Stevie Wonder and other "softer" rock musicians of today, that many listeners find comforting and uplifting. Nevertheless, for learning and self-exploration, classical music has proven to engage more of the brain and reach deeper into the psyche. According to Lozanov,

> *The structural principles of a classical composition exert their influence through a humane philosophy, expressed in a perfect form. They create within human beings the necessary conditions for a natural transition from chaos and disharmony towards order, harmony, consistency, logic, inspiration, and delight. These principles create also the conditions needed for a regulation of the naturally arising psycho-relaxation, the state of mind where reserve capacities are revealed and tapped.*[5]

For as many rock fans who defend the music, there are more—the vast majority of young parents—who are beginning to become deeply concerned about the music their children are listening to. To them, the music seems to become more disturbing with each passing year.

Their youngsters point out that the Beatles offended *their* parents' ears, and that jazz offended their grandparents' ears. It seems that people always resist new sounds. In fact, the later, more complex music of Beethoven was not accepted by his society.

Our ears can get used to almost any new sounds if we hear them long enough. But those sounds are not necessarily beneficial to our systems. We must learn to discriminate between sounds that are rejected simply because they are different, and sounds that are detrimental to our well-being.

In the movie, *Back to the Future,* when the main character plays a modern rock guitar solo for a 1960's audience, all the teenagers hold their hands over their ears. Their systems could not handle such sounds. Our young people may believe that they can handle them today, but according to recent scientific research, some of the most pressing crises of our day may be exacerbated by the chaotic, frantic music we hear around us all the time.

According to John Diamond, an Australian born physician who practices in New York State, many young people who have become addicted to rock music suffer a reversal of their value systems, so that they will unconsciously choose that which is damaging to them. He is concerned that certain kinds of rock music engender self-destructive and suicidal tendencies in many teenagers and young adults. Laurel Keyes elaborates on this in her book, "Toning":

> *When the body is under constant stress it may become addicted to the adrenaline flow, as with any drug, and feel the need of it. Many people are 'hooked' on this sense of agitation and become adrenaline junkies. They think that they cannot work or study without that stimulation, but the tension in the body (and drain on the pancreas) takes its toll. It weakens or destroys the body as any addiction destroys through enslavement.*[6]

Parents approach me at workshops with anxiety about the negative influence that disturbing rock music may be having on their children. They want to know how they can provide a healthier musical environment. They are also concerned about the growing number of cases of hearing loss due to the loudness of the music, and about the negative influence of so-called satanic lyrics. But according to modern scientists, the most harmful effect of certain chaotic rock music is its beat.

Dr. Diamond works with musicians to help them improve the quality of their performances. His life's work is to research the life energy in music. He has found that music has the capacity to strengthen or weaken our life energy. He claims that certain kinds of rock music have a debilitating effect on our systems.[7] This particular music has an *anapestic* beat, in which the last beat of the measure is stressed and there is a slight stop before the first beat begins again. This rhythm is counter to the body's natural organic rhythm, which is more of a waltz beat in which the first beat of the measure is accented, and the rhythm is regular.

Diamond believes that our bodies can tell the difference between these sounds that strengthen us and those that weaken us. With certain chaotic rock music, the body enters a state of alarm that causes a great deal of stress. This leads to hyperactivity and restlessness in children. Their nerves become strained and a pseudo-energy ensues which often results in a state of fatigue and malaise later on. Dr. Diamond found that many schoolchildren's grades improved considerably after they stopped using rock as background music for homework.[8]

When I was teaching junior high students to speak Spanish using Lozanov's system of stress-free language learning, I noticed that the children came into class each morning at 8:00 a.m. feeling exhausted. I asked them what they were eating for breakfast. Most were eating healthy foods. Then I asked them what music they were listening to in the morning. Many mentioned several Heavy Metal rock groups. I suggested that they listen to classical music for just one week and notice if they felt more energetic during the day. The students who did found that they felt much better.

There have been numerous studies done comparing the effect of various kinds of music on humans, animals and even plants. It is commonly accepted now that plants respond positively to classical music.

Dorothy Retallack is a professional musician who performed a well-known series of experiments involving plants and music. At Temple Buell College in Colorado in 1970, she compared the growth of plants exposed to classical music to those exposed to acid rock music. Using corn, squash, petunias, zinneas and marigolds, she found that plants subjected to hard rock began to turn away from the radio, the source of the sound. They seemed to need more water than usual, and by the 16th day of the experiment almost all the marigolds had died.

In an experiment with squash, Retallack reported:

> *The squash in the classical chamber had grown toward the radio and was beginning to twine itself around it, while in the rock chamber it had grown in the opposite direction and looked as if it was trying to climb the wall.*[9]

This experiment led Retallack to wonder if the growth of adolescents, like plants, might be affected by music. She felt that adolescence was a time when the emotional nature of young people "should be calmed down" rather than over-stimulated by the strong percussive beat of rock music. Ironically, the plants loved the Indian classical music of Ravi Shankar, another favorite of adolescents of that era, so much that they wrapped themselves completely around the speakers. Plants apparently have no cultural bias.

A recent study of the neurological response of mice to different kinds of musical rhythms revealed that discordant sounds disrupt learning and alter brain tissue. Gevasia M. Schreckenberg, a neurobiologist at Georgian Court College, and Harvey H. Bird, a physicist at Fairleigh Dickinson University, had heard critics of rock music charge that the music was damaging the brains of young people. They decided to find out if it was true.

In a recent magazine article on the experiment, it was reported that "mice exposed day and night to an incessant drumbeat not only developed difficulties in learning and memory as compared with a control group, but they also incurred structural changes in their brain cells. The neurons showed signs of wear and tear from stress."[10]

In an eight-week period, mice exposed to the insistent sounds of perpetual drumming had a much more difficult time going through a maze to find their food than the mice who listened to Strauss waltzes. After a three-week respite, the disharmonic groups could not remember how to get their food, while the other group found it easily.

When examining their brain tissue, Schreckenberg found that there was abnormal growth of neurons in the hippocampus, a structure associated with alertness, learning and memory. She also found abnormal amounts of messenger RNA, a chemical vital to memory storage.

The two researchers concluded that the rhythm of the music reduced memory capacity by disturbing the rhythm of the brainwaves–known as theta waves–in the hippocampus, and could lead to short-term memory loss. They speculate that these erratic growth patterns in neurons can cause serious learning disabilities later on. If the brains of mice react this way to jarring rhythms, it is very possible that our own human thought processes could be disrupted too.

Diamond claims that in human beings, the stress of destructive music causes not only a loss of energy, negativity and depression, isolation, hopelessness and aggressive behavior, but disorientation and confusion. The stress in the body causes an effect in the brain that Diamond calls "switching," in which the left and right hemispheres of the brain are thrown off-balance. The left hemisphere becomes dominant, resulting in subtle difficulties in perception and other manifestations of stress. We revert to a primitive pattern of neurological organization. Our reptilian, or old animal brain, takes over. The repetition of the mechanical beat, resounding in our ears over and over again, requires mostly the participation of the instinctive part of our brain which specializes in routine and ritual.[11]

For the most part, there is little feeling in this kind of music and, consequently, no healing. The music is unable to reach the areas of the brain that respond to emotional stimulation.

As a result, Dr. Diamond found that children's thought patterns become confused, they make more mistakes, and they find it more difficult to access their creativity. Their thinking becomes robotic and their schoolwork suffers.

Adults who listen to chaotic rock music are unable to work as productively; they make more errors and have more difficulty making decisions. When both children and adults begin to study or work with classical music, their work improves markedly because the music energizes them. It helps them think clearly, rather than disorienting them and clouding their perceptions.[12]

What can we do about our children's addiction to rock music? The worst thing we can do is to suddenly confiscate all their albums of Nirvana and Pearl Jam. If, in fact, heavy rock music is an aural drug, they may experience more aggression without it as they go into withdrawal. Their resistance will go up immediately and become a wall between you, resulting in them never wanting to try "your music."

I have found that the best thing we can do to help children discover the power and beauty of classical music is to simply expose them to it. Play it at home and in the classroom. They will be taking it in subconsciously even if they are not consciously listening to it.

My own children have listened to classical music at home all of their lives. All of them are also avid rock music fans (though not hard rock), but my oldest son recently asked for Beethoven, Chopin and Bach recordings for his birthday.

My middle son loves his *Nutcracker Suite* as much as some of his rock music, and my youngest son has a special penchant for *Come Sweet Death* by J. S. Bach when he feels like crawling into his inner space. All of them love the Chopin waltzes because they grew up listening to me play them on the piano.

If children are never exposed to the enriching nourishment of classical music, how can they learn to love it and use it in their lives to further their personal growth process? James Galway, one of the world's greatest flutists, remarked, "Despite all my education at music colleges and conservatories and work with the great orchestras, it was our music at home which had the strongest influence on my life and career."

Recently, many of us have begun to take more responsibility for our own attitudes, beliefs and value systems. People are healing physical and emotional illness by surrounding themselves with positive, uplifting thought patterns. Music can help foster the values we cherish. If we truly desire a state of health, well-being, and spiritual blossoming, we will honor the power of music to bring it to us by listening to and exposing our children to the music that will benefit them rather than accepting the dictates of an addictive society.

What to Use and How to Use It

If you are reluctant to use classical music because you don't know anything about it and you don't have any in your home, you can begin with a small collection of six or seven masterpieces from several different periods of music. If you know the characteristics of the music of each period, it will help you decide when and how to use each piece of music. The periods of music used primarily for learning and self-discovery are the Baroque, Classical, Romantic and Impressionistic.

Baroque music (1600-1750) is highly structured and precise. It has an energetic movement and steady pulsation that keeps you from getting tired. It is dependable and predictable and makes you feel secure and ordered. The music is emotional and dramatic with "the capacity to organize a thousand details into a monumental, overpowering whole," according to musicologist Joseph Machlis.[6]

For this reason, it is very effective for whole brain integration. A few examples of major Baroque composers are Bach, Handel, Vivaldi and Corelli. The music of Bach, in particular, combines feeling and precision in such a masterful way that it can be used for almost any purpose you have in mind.

With the *Classical* period (1750-1820), the harmonic aspect of music was further developed, utilizing frequent changes of tone color or timbre. This style is characterized by an effortless continuity, clarity and poise. Whereas in the Baroque period there were even contrasts of loud and soft dynamics, the Classical era experimented with sudden changes and surprises in accent and dynamics, so that the rhythmic patterns are more flexible.

This makes the music effective for stimulating associations in the brain, triggering memories and piquing creativity. Machlis calls the Classical period a time of "ordered beauty." A few outstanding composers of this period are Haydn, Mozart and Beethoven.

The *Romantic* style (1820-1900) is characterized by a sense of individualism and uniqueness. It is a highly personal music and has strong emotional polarities. It is like an outpouring of feelings, so it naturally helps you pour out your own feelings. According to Machlis, it contains the picturesque, fantastic and macabre and has lyricism with emotional appeal. A few major composers of this period are Brahms, Mendelssohn, late Beethoven, Tchaikovsky, Schumann, Wagner and Rachmaninoff.

Impressionistic music (late nineteenth and early twentieth century) has a dream-like style and a certain fluidity of movement. It is very powerful for evoking images because of its many changes in tone color and subtle nuances of mood. If you or your children have never experienced music imaging, you can begin with music from this period. It may elicit more visual images than other kinds of music. Examples of composers from the Impressionistic period are Debussy, Respighi, and Ravel.

Most modern classical music is not used for learning or self-exploration because of its dissonant, anti-therapeutic sounds. Lozanov uses no modern composers at all, not even the Impressionists. The music of Vaughan Williams, Aaron Copland and other modern composers whose compositions resolve harmonically are used in GIM and are considered therapeutic by Dr. Bonny.

The chart at the end of this chapter is designed to help you start your own collection of classical music. It is based on my research, supplemented by the work of Dr. Lozanov, Dr. Bonny and Hal Lingerman. It describes the period in which each piece was composed, its general effect on the human system, suggestions for its use, and its therapeutic value. There is also space for you to write in your own response.

Music Activity #9
Tuning in to Your Choice

Listen to one of the five pieces of music suggested in Chapter One. Choose a second piece of music of another genre: country & western, jazz, new age, pop or other. Ask yourself these questions:

o Does this music relax me?

o Does it energize me? Do I still feel energetic a few hours later?

○ Do I feel emotionally balanced when I listen to it?

○ Does it help me integrate my intellectual and feeling sides?

○ Do my perceptions seem sharper?

○ Does the music bring me thoughts and images of beauty?

○ Does it make me feel creative?

○ Do I feel myself being physically, mentally or spiritually stimulated?

There are many other questions you could add to these, depending on your own personal value system. The people I work with experiment with different pieces of music, noticing which music is most effective. But it is advisable to work first with the music that has been researched and proven to be effective, and then experiment on your own.

The table on the next page provides a list of pieces, and the therapeutic value each is shown to have.

Music Activity #10:
Music Selection Chart

Musical Selection	Period of Music	General Effect	Possible Uses	Response
Pachelbel: Canon in D	Baroque	calming, provides structure & grounding balancing energizing	study story telling resting	
Bach: Brandenburg Concertos	Baroque	calming, balancing creative writing or projects energizing sharpens mental powers	study/memorization reading information aloud	
Vivaldi: The Four Seasons	Baroque	energizing tranquilizing motivating uplifting	for low energy periods play in the morning to set the tone for the day silent work time	
Beethoven: Symphony No. 6, ("Pastorale")	Classical	exhilarating, stirs creativity Music Imaging stimulates imagination awakens tenderness, feelings of beauty, nature	story telling or reading	
Mozart: Eine Kleine Nachtmusik	Classical	uplifting, energizing conducting, movement inspiring motivating	use especially with children for motivation for adventure–type imagery	
Handel: The Water Music	Baroque	energizing centering structure	study and focus story telling/reading	
Respighi: The Pines of Rome	Impressionistic	dreamy evokes imagery stimulates fantasy	Music Imaging activities drawing creative writing	

Music Activity #11
Performers and Labels

Here are some of the major labels which distribute classical music. The quality of the recording strongly affects the final sound. The labels listed below are known for their high recording standards and rosters of gifted, well-known performers:

Angel	EMI	Naxos
Chandos	Koch	Odyssey
Columbia	London	Philips
Deutsche Grammophon	Mercury	RCA

For further assistance in determining the highest quality tapes, records or compact discs to buy, consult *The Healing Energies of Music* by Hal A. Lingerman. You can often buy good quality older recordings at very reasonable prices.

Music Activity #12
New Age, Ancient and Ethnic Music List

The following list features music chosen by Sara Jane Stokes, Ph.D., R.M.T., B.C., (my co-facilitator for Advanced GIM trainings) which I have found to be especially relaxing and centering. The music is usually soothing by nature rather than motivating, so it has a calming rather than a stimulating effect. As with other types of music, monitor your body's response to each piece before assuming that it is having a positive effect on you.

David Darling	*Eight String Religion*
	The Tao of Cello
Deuter	*Land of Enchantment*
	Cicada
Philip Elcano	*Rain Dance*
James Galway	*The Enchanted Forest*
	Melodies of Japan
Jan Garbarek	*Officium*

Kay Gardner	*A Rainbow Path*
Harmonic Choir	*Harmonic Choir, Vol. 1-3*
Paul Horn	*Inside the Taj Mahal*
	The Great Pyramid
Michael Jones	*After the Rain*
	Magical Child
Peter Kater	*Migration*
Georgia Kelly	*Seapeace*
Daniel Kobialka	*Path of Joy*
	Dream Passage
	Going Home
	When You Wish Upon a Star
David Lanz, Paul Speers	*Natural States*
Carlos Nakai	*Island of Bows*
Narada Artists	*A Childhood Remembered*
Richard Souther	*Vision—Music of Hildegard von Bingen*
Alan Stivel	*Renaissance of the Celtic Harp*
Windham Hill Records	*In Search of Angels*
Danny Wright	*Phantasys*

Also useful are recordings of environmental sounds, such as *Bamboo Waterfall* (Nature Recordings of Wind Chimes and Bells), *Mountain Streams* with music from pan flute and Celtic harp—*Sounds of Nature* (Silver Bells Music, Nashville, Tennessee), *Tibetan Bells* by Henry Wolff and Nancy Hennings, and *The Environmental Series.*

Music Activity #13
Noticing Your Body's Response

o Find a place to lie down, or find a comfortable place to sit.

o Close your eyes and notice how your body is feeling. Notice if you feel tired or energetic. Be aware of any parts of your body that feel tense or any muscles that have tightened up. Listen to your heart beating. You might even want to take your pulse. Notice if your body feels particularly heavy or light, or if there is any pain or discomfort any-where. Notice how you are breathing; whether you are taking short, shallow breaths or longer, deeper breaths.

o Turn on the Pachelbel Canon in D, which often relieves stress.

o Take a few deep breaths and allow yourself to be immersed in the music. When the music has ended, notice any changes you feel in your body.

o Compare how you feel now with how you felt before you turned on the music.

o Try a more physically stimulating piece of music, such as *Eine Kleine Nachtmusik*. Notice your body's response to this kind of music. Be aware of any parts of your body that may want to move and let your-self do that. After the music is over, notice any changes in energy or motivation.

Music Activity #14
Muscle Testing to Music

o For this activity, work with a friend or family member. Ask your part-ner to extend their left arm straight out (if they are right-handed). Place your left hand on their right shoulder to anchor, as you push down on their left arm just above the wrist. Push down firmly. Then let go. If your partner's arm springs back up again, they are strong. If you can easily push their arm down, their muscle has weakened.

o Switch and let your partner test you.

o Now try it with music. Using the selections below, or any music you have at home that you would like to test out, turn on each piece for two or three minutes before testing. Stand, facing your partner, and test their muscle strength. Then switch and have them test yours. Jot down the results (strong, weaker, weak.)

Sample Selections

Pachelbel   *Canon in D*

Vangelis   *Chariots of Fire*

Steven Halpern   *Spectrum Suite*

Any piece of heavy metal rock music

J. Strauss   *On The Beautiful Blue Danube*

                                            Tales from the Vienna Woods

Even though there is a tendency for certain music to weaken or strengthen our muscles, each person may react differently to a certain piece of music. The purpose of this activity is simply to have you notice how your body responds to different pieces of music quite independently of your personal likes and dislikes.

Although you have not isolated the variables, such as the particular recording, conductor or performer, digital or analog recording, and this is not a true laboratory test, you may be astonished at what happens. At my workshops, many people have found that their muscles sometimes weaken with pieces of music they really like. Conversely, their muscles are strengthened by music they usually do not care for or listen to regularly. Your body may have a different idea of what is good for you!

Notes

1. Verny, Thomas, and Kelly, John, *The Secret Life of the Unborn Child*. Dell (New York), 1981, p. 34.

2. Hamel, Peter, *Through Music to the Self*. Scherz Verlag (Berne, W. Germany) 1976.

3. From a lecture by Dr. Georgi Lozanov, May 17, 1979, in Orinda, CA.

4. Halpern, Steven, with Savary, Louis, *Sound Health*. Harper & Row (New York), 1985, p.49.

5. Lozanov, Georgi, *The Foreign Language Teacher's Suggestopedic Manual*. Gordon and Breach (New York), 1988, p.70.

6. Keyes, Laurel, *Toning*. DeVorss & Co. (Marina del Rey, CA), 1973, p. 115.

7. Diamond, John, *Your Body Doesn't Lie*. Warner Books (New York), 1980, p. 161–163.

8. Ibid., p.164.

9. Retallack, Dorothy, *The Sound of Music and Plants.* DeVorss & Co. (Marina Del Rey, CA), 1973, p. 19.

10. Lipkin, Richard, *"Jarring Music Takes Toll on Mice."* Insight, April 4, 1988, p. 58.

11. Diamond, John, *Your Body Doesn't Lie.* Warner Books (New York), 1980, p. 164–165.

12. Ibid., p. 164–165.

13. See Chapter 6 on John Diamond's work with muscle testing.

Music and Healing

Today, like every other day, we wake up empty and frightened. Don't open the door to the study and begin reading. Take down the dulcimer. Let the beauty we love be what we do. There are hundreds of ways to kneel and kiss the ground.

-Rumi

Ignoring the power of music and sound and its profound effects on us can be not only unhealthy but dangerous. Psychologist Roberto Assagioli, author of *Psychosynthesis,* believes music can facilitate the development of our highest potential as human beings or it can plunge us into despair and depression and even cause disease. He says:

As is well known, sound has great power over inorganic matter. By means of sound it is possible to cause geometric figures to form on sand and also to cause objects to be shattered. How much more powerful, then, must be the impact of this force on the vibrating, living substance of our sensitive bodies![1]

Music is this powerful because much of our response to it occurs below the level of consciousness. We are usually not aware that our pulse speeds up with the rhythm of a certain piece of music, or that a certain melodic pattern may trigger the memory of an open field we used to play in as children.

Our Hidden Responses to Music

Although our responses to music may not come up into conscious awareness, they still affect us subconsciously. Because the images that arise from the music do not involve critical analysis, they are absorbed automatically and directly. As a result, they penetrate much more deeply into our consciousness. We might suddenly feel frazzled or tense, tearful or playful, without ever knowing what brought on those feelings.

Unless we begin to notice what the music we listen to is doing to our bodies, our brains, our psyches and our spirits, we can easily let ourselves be manipulated by it. Advertisers have long known and understood the power of music, and they use it to persuade customers to buy their products.

Lately, they seem to have become quite knowledgeable about classical music, using it wisely and well. A commercial for a computer, for example, appropriately uses a Bach two-part invention. The precise, highly organized structure of this music focuses the mind and is a bridge to the highly ordered world of the computer. *The Tchaikovsky Violin Concerto* or a *Brahms* symphony simply would not be as fitting. Unconsciously, the right music creates an affinity with the product that we would not consciously choose.

In my Music Imaging workshops, I have often asked participants if, while shopping in a store or dining in a restaurant where music was playing in the background, they had ever felt anxious, irritable or headachy. At least half of the group usually groans and nods their heads in assent. Many of them never realized that the music being played in the store possibly caused their irritation. Others suspected so, but just kept on shopping, tolerating the bad feelings.

Not one of them had ever approached the management and pleasantly asked them to change the music or turn it off. One or two had asked them to lower the volume, not realizing that it is largely the beat of the music that frazzles the nerves. None of them expressed their anxiety about their inability to focus on their shopping chores to the store manager.

I have also presented music for stress management at various health spas where chaotic rock music is often played during exercise classes. I have found that most of the women feel jarred and upset by the music, yet they say nothing. They assume they are simply out of touch with what is "in" and they resign themselves to whatever they hear around them.

Music has this much influence on our lives for a very good reason: we are music. We live and breathe in sound. Not only do we live in it, but it lives in us as well. At any given moment, your body could be responding to many different sounds simultaneously without your ever knowing it: the hum of your refrigerator, the beeping and screeching of traffic noises through the window, the sputtering of a neighbor's lawn mower—as well as the soothing strains of a violin concerto flowing out of your radio. Since our physical bodies are resonators, we are always responding to the vibrational patterns around us.

These sounds resonate through us, whether we notice them or not. Dr. Randall McClellan, director of the Sonic Arts Foundation, speaks of the substance of the body as a "virtual symphony of frequencies, sounds, and biological, mental and emotional rhythms in a state of continuous flow, which seek to achieve and maintain the state of perfect balance and equilibrium."[2]

The implications of this concept are profound. The quantum physicists, beginning with Max Planck and his theory of quanta in 1900 and Einstein, with his theory of relativity in 1905, and continuing with the work of David Bohm, Fritjof Capra and others, have found that matter is really energy, and energy, of course, is vibration.[3]

The "old physics" or Newtonian view explained reality in terms of the atom as a solid particle that combines with other atoms to form physical matter. Mass and energy were seen as two separate systems, and the world was perceived as one big machine. Quantum theory, on the other hand, postulates that matter is in a constant state of motion or flux. Physicists John Schwarz of Cal Tech and Michael Green of Queen Mary College in London have found that:

> *The fundamental particles of the universe are tiny snips of subatomic vibrating particle strings 100 billion times shorter than the diameter of the nucleus of an atom. These particle strings vibrate in pre-determined ways and interact with one another to create the properties of the particles of matter. Matter then emerges as a kind of subatomic music unifying all the forces of nature, including gravitational force, in one simple theory.*[4]

We are in a continual state of becoming. So is music. We both originate from the same unmanifest state of absolute silence and stillness, from which all energy, sound, and vibration emanates.

If the universe is in a continual state of transformation, then so-called coincidences such as the phenomenon Jung calls *synchronicity*, or unexplained incidences of ESP, as well as time distortion while listening to a piece of music, can be understood within the context of quantum physics. Since everything in the universe is connected to and interdependent on everything else, the whole suffers when the parts are treated as separate items in potential conflict with each other, as in the mechanistic worldview.

Through this new "open systems" approach, our whole arena of potentialities and probabilities becomes a reality. *In The Dancing Wu Li Masters*, Gary Zukav offers his definition of reality:

> *'Reality' is what we take to be true. What we take to be true is what we believe. What we believe is based upon our perceptions. What we perceive depends upon what we look for. What we look for depends upon what we think, What we think depends upon what we perceive. What we perceive determines what we believe. What we believe determines what we take to be*

true. What we take to be true is our reality.[5]

Despite evidence that reality is created internally, human understanding is still set in the concrete belief that only the logical and the material aspects of life are real. It is still difficult for our minds to validate anything we cannot measure with the outer eye. Yet this immaterial force called music can heal, uplift, calm, enlighten, nourish and strengthen. We cannot see it do these things, nor can we explain how it can do them. Yet the effects are visible. According to physicist Brian Swimme:

> *When we listen to music, we are entering a patterned energy field and our eardrums move in resonance with these patterns of energy. Fluctuations initiated by the violinist actually shape everything, violin strings, violin wood, air, ears. If there's music around, everything is moved by it, humans as well as window panes. We think of the drummer as playing the drum only; in truth, the drummer is playing the world.*[6]

As we become more attuned to our inner selves, we invite the invisible to create the shapes and forms and colors of our consciousness. This book is concerned with the quest to connect these subconscious influences to our conscious minds. As we begin to do this, we inevitably choose the music that benefits us, that helps us grow and develop healthy bodies and whole personalities.

Einstein Meets Pythagoras

Long ago, music was used as a therapeutic tool for balance and harmony. The ancients knew, by way of "direct knowing" or intuition, the significance of music and sound. It was understood that illness was not just a physical phenomenon. For example, it is said that the ancient Chinese emperors would send wise men to visit villages and listen to the music being played. By noting how close the sounds came to the ancient Chinese pitch, the emperor would determine whether there would be war or peace, plenty or pestilence. The music was an indicator of the economic and political condition of the village.

Confucius believed that music had a great influence on the mental state and therefore the political and psychological ambience of a whole nation. He wrote:

> *When a somber and depressing type of music prevails, we know the people are distressed and sorrowful. When a languorous, easy type of music with many long-drawn out airs prevail, we know the people are peaceful and happy. When a strong and forceful type of music prevails, beginning with a full display of sounds, we know that the people are hearty and strong. When a pure, pious, and majestic type of music prevails, we know that the people are pious; when a gentle, lucid and quietly progressing type of music prevails, we know that the people are kind and affectionate. When lewd, exciting and upsetting music prevails, we know that the people are immoral. When the climate deteriorates, animal and plant life degenerate, and when the world is chaotic, the rituals and music become licentious. We find then a type of music that is rueful without restraint and joyous without calm. Therefore, the superior man tries to create harmony in the human heart by a rediscovery of human nature, and tries to promote music as a means to the perfection of human culture. When such music prevails and the peoples' minds are led toward the right ideals and aspirations, we may see the appearance of a great nation.*

The ancient Greeks, as well, had great respect for music. Pythagoras understood what classroom teachers are now realizing: that certain sequences of chords can actually change behavior. He saw the universe as a musical instrument. He believed in a cosmic vibration that could enter the being through the mind. One in tune with this cosmic vibration was a healthy person.

These vibrations cannot be consciously heard; they may include grass growing or the sun moving across the sky or the stars twinkling. But we are affected by them nevertheless. When we feel irritable or out-of-sorts, we are likely to be out of tune with this cosmic vibration. When things feel just right, there is a deep knowing that we are aligned to it. Often people feel that alignment when they are surrounded by nature's beauty, or even imagining a nature scene in their minds.

To Pythagoras, the whole world was held together by sound. He connected the distances between the planets with the musical intervals between tones. He called this the "Music of the Spheres." Two thousand years later, in 1619, Johann Kepler, a mathematician and astronomer, calculated the musical intervals for the then-known six planets and the moon. According to Dr. Randall McClellan, Kepler

> ...*worked out a system for determining the proper pitch, the proper octave for each planet, and the speed at which each planet would slowly change from its fundamental pitch to the indicated interval pitch and back again according to the planets' distance from the sun.*[7]

How can vibration affect us even when we can't hear it? In ancient Eastern civilizations, people could feel the effect of vibrations in the powerful energy centers of their bodies they called *chakras*. It was believed that the universe had been created out of a spiritual vibration that came from the Source of all things. Healing with music was a highly respected science based on the use of vibration. Sacred chants, hypnotic rhythms and ancient melodic patterns were used to awaken the chakras.

As ancient wisdom blends with modern physics, we are beginning to understand, in scientific and mathematical terms, what was always intuited and.felt by great philosophers and sages.

In the 1930's the Swiss sound researcher, Hans Jenny, discovered that when sand and metal filings were vibrated on metal dishes at certain frequencies, they formed themselves into shapes similar to common patterns in nature, such as those in honeycombs or nautilus shells. In developing his new science of *cymatics,* the study of the interrelationship of waveforms with matter, he confirmed that "everything is generated and sustained by vibration."

The modern cosmologist and physicist, Brian Swimme, speaks of music as the great mover of the universe, and claims that cosmologists of our times have discovered that even the galaxies themselves originated from music.

The fireball at the beginning of time is a huge molten ball ringing with music. When we hear fireball, we think, perhaps, of a flame. In reality, the fireball is many times denser than steel. Chords of energy resonated throughout the fireball like music vibrating through a great cosmic ball. These patterns of music organized the fireball into complex forms, forms that would receive the name, some fifteen billion years later, of galaxy. A galaxy is a chord of music from the fireball, now expressed in a new form.

An amazing story. The music of the fireball becomes galaxies, becomes stars, becomes meadowlarks, humans and whales. Even more: had there been no music in the fireball, the fireball would have simply dispersed without creating galaxies. We are learning that music is the efficacious power of the universe. No wonder the deepest realms of the human spirit come alive with music. No wonder we hunger to create music. No wonder we realize that until our lives are devoted to musical celebrations, human society will continue its needless suffering.[8]

Our Inner Harmony

As we become aware of what inner harmony feels like, we also become more aware of the uncomfortable tension of disharmony and discord within us. With our growing sensitivity to these vibrations, we begin to choose the harmonious in our lives and avoid the discord that isolates us from our natural universe. Pythagoras advised people to begin and end each day with music. He claimed it liberates the listener from the day's conflicts and concerns and enables him or her to sleep more soundly and dream more vividly.

We rarely think about what we listen to when we go to sleep in the evening and much less about what we awaken to in the morning. News of world disasters, hard rock, endless commercial jingles assail our ears. We take them into our bodies and psyches without really understanding how deeply they affect us. Try using classical music to begin and end your day—and notice the difference.

In his book *The Healing Energies of Music*, Hal Lingerman suggests the bright, airy sounds of Vivaldi's flute concertos or Telemann's string compositions for waking up. For falling asleep, Lingerman recommends Meditation from *Thaïs* by Massenet, *"The Children's Prayer"* from Hansel and Gretel by Humperdinck, and *Bach-Kobialka: Jesu, Joy of Man's Desiring,* among others.[9]

I often wake up to Haydn string quartets. They get me out of bed gently with their stimulating energy. People who are not "morning people" may feel a little too stimulated with these. A cassette tape recommended by Linda Keiser for attuning to the day is *Morning Moods* by Deutsche Grammophon. The selection from Grieg's *Peer Gynt Suite,* also called *"Morning Mood,"* feels like slow stretching, or the sun gradually rising. *The Mozart Flute* and Harp Concerto, especially the slow movement, usually lulls me to sleep.

Since our response to music is very personal, these pieces may have a different effect on you, but the experience will broaden your sensitivity to the different ways music can make you feel.

Music Activity #15
The Music of Harmony

In my workshops I read a story I have written called *The Riversea Goddess* to specially selected music. The story is about a mythical kingdom ruled by the beautiful Goddess Azurebella and what happens when a disruptive, abandoned baby dragon floats into the harbor of the idyllic island. The language used stimulates all the senses. When read together with music, a powerful physical and emotional climate is created that has often brought out surprising responses in participants. Long-held angers, sorrows, and conflicts deeply buried often surface after the story is heard. In order to experience your own personal response:

1. You may read the story silently or aloud.

2. You may read the story to Beethoven's *Symphony No. 6, "Pastoral."*

3. A tape of the story read to music can be ordered on last page of this book. Music, story and voice are orchestrated to evoke a powerful response from the unconscious. Listen in a relaxed position with your eyes closed, noticing the feelings and images that come up.

As you listen to the story, notice how your body is feeling. Be aware of any changes in your muscle tension, heartbeat, circulation or breathing. Notice any colors or shapes that come to mind. Notice any changes in your emotions or feelings. Notice if you feel sad or angry, joyful or peaceful. Be aware of any memories the music and story are bringing to you. Notice any new ideas or insights that may come up. Write them down or draw your impressions spontaneously—artistic talent is not required. You don't have to be a Michaelangelo. Simply let yourself express in your own way the experience the story and music brings to you.

The Riversea Goddess

In ancient times there lived a highly sensitive goddess called Azurebella. She was half human and half divine. Whatever she saw or smelled or felt became part of her. As she strolled through the sweet-smelling gardens of the kingdom her skin took in the fragrance of fresh roses and jasmine perfume, which, in turn, permeated the whole kingdom. When she set her dreamy eyes upon a peaceful meadow, lush and green with trees of ripe, delicious fruit, you could look into her eyes days later and gaze upon this lovely scene. You could even taste the fruit.

Every morning, Azurebella went down to the riversea to bathe. As she splashed about in the clear, fresh water, the ting of tiny bells was heard throughout the kingdom. Thunderous voices joined in as the powerful waves of the sea cleansed her whole being and the waterfall rinsed her hair.

While Azurebella bathed in the pure riversea, the people of the kingdom could not help but be bathed in the song that resonated with her pure heart. At the same time, all the sounds around her were reflected in the people with perfect clarity. Soon all the hearts were beating to the rhythm of the waves breaking on the shore. The people naturally felt like singing.

Each person sang out his own special tone with all his heart, and although every tone sounded different, together they blended into a majesty that matched the sounds of the wind and the rain and the earth moving in its orbit. And so there was perfect peace in the kingdom.

Life went on like that for centuries until one day, while bathing in the riversea, Azurebella spied a raft floating on the water. Lying on the raft was the biggest baby dragon she had ever seen. It had been born on a far away island and didn't seem to know where it was going.

As soon as the baby dragon saw land, it jumped clumsily off the raft and, with a great crash, it landed in the riversea not more than ten feet away from Azurebella. The dragon was very angry at its parents for abandoning it and it started to cry and scream as it kicked the waves and made them foam with anger too. Then it kept pounding its foot on the riversea floor while it flailed about wildly.

In a flash, all the people felt their hearts reverse their beat and begin to pound like the dragon's foot. Their special tones were lost in this new wilderness. It felt as if all the different parts of them had separated and gotten lost and couldn't find each other.

Most people were crying with loneliness, but there were some who started to follow the baby dragon wherever it went, wildly jumping and pounding along with it whenever it had its tantrums. Soon they began to have tantrums too, and when they wanted to stop jumping and pounding, they just could not. Even after the dragon went to sleep at night, the pounding went on and on inside their heads and they could never hear anything else. After awhile they became very sick and no one knew how to help them.

Finally, the Riversea Goddess could stand no more. She approached them and offered them her ancient wisdom. Although she was not at all sure they would accept it, she gave them a golden disk that had the power to put the dragon to sleep for seven days. During that time, they could bathe in the peaceful riversea sounds once again and notice how they felt.

All of the dragon's followers accepted, and the very next day they plunged into the riversea. The goddess's sweet voice beckoned to them and they followed, allowing the gentle, lilting waves to carry them along wherever they were going. The waters swished back and forth, soothing their spirits.

As soon as the pounding stopped, they heard a beautiful hum that seemed to be coming from beneath the riversea. They dove down, down into its depths and they were immersed in the most enchanting sounds they had ever heard. When they came up to the surface, the waves nudged them gently to the shore. They felt calm and well again and joined hands with the other group that had been so lonely, and all were in harmony once more.

When the baby dragon awoke, seven days later, he heard— really heard, for the first time—the sound of the riversea, and the harmony of Azurebella's subjects, and his tail, which had started to twitch and flail, grew quiet, and the roar which had formed in his throat dissolved. He felt, for the very first time, what it was to be in harmony with the earth and the riversea and other living creatures, and he found his own tone to sing as he joined all of the people of the kingdom in their universal song.

♪ ♪ ♪

Using the following guidelines, jot down your impressions.

- Was there a difference in the way you perceived the story when you first read it to yourself and then when you read it or heard it read aloud with music?
- What changes did you notice in your physiological functions (breathing, pulse rate, muscle tension)?
- Where did you feel the music in your body?
- Were you more relaxed after listening than before?

o How did the story/music energize you?

o What changes of mood or emotion did you notice?

o Did the conflict in the story touch any conflicts in your current life?

o Did the music suggest a way of resolving them?

o How did you feel about the baby dragon? How did you image him?

o Draw the dragon.

o Draw Azurebella.

For an added dimension, do this activity with a family member or friend. Share your drawings, feelings and thoughts. You may discover interesting aspects of this person that you were never aware of before.

(A special note on the optional *Riversea Goddess* story tape: Many people find that listening to this tape relaxes their tensions and brings them a feeling of harmony and joy. The first time you hear the tape, the music may carry you deep into your own unconscious. You may well stop listening consciously to the story, but it is nonetheless affecting you on levels below the conscious. A second playing of the tape allows you to listen to the story more consciously.)

Responses

When I read the story in my workshop the participants respond in many different ways. The emotional and physical responses often engender an unexpected therapeutic effect. A young man in his twenties was surprised to find how stirred he was by the story and music.

Having settled down into the story, he could feel the peace and harmony of Azurebella's kingdom. He allowed his conscious thoughts to be submerged, and unconscious feelings and concerns began to float up to the surface. He started to get in touch with his feelings of insecurity with regard to his marriage. When the dragon came into the picture, the man could feel his heart beating much faster. He also felt his muscles tighten, and there was a knot in his stomach. His mind began to drift. Suddenly, he found himself re-experiencing the conflict he had been having with his wife that week. He could actually feel the anger, frustration and fatigue it had caused him.

They had been married just a year. She was newly pregnant and had only that morning expressed a wish to go back to see her parents for two or three weeks. The girl's parents were well-to-do: her father a doctor, her mother head of her own design firm. The young man had taken his wife 3,000 miles away from their luxurious home on Long Island because he believed the parents, and especially the mother, had a tremendous influence on his wife.

He had just opened a small electronics repair shop; his hours were long, his income uncertain. The .baby had not been planned for, and there had been friction between himself and his wife. But he loved her very much and was afraid that, once she returned to her old home and doting parents, she might not come back to the marriage.

As the music and story moved out of conflict and tension into a moment of resolution, he saw the problem from a distance. From this perspective he could see the standpoints of all four people involved. And he realized that his wife's love for him was as strong as his for her, and that the knowledge of a grandchild, and his willingness to have his wife share a few weeks with her parents, would create a warmth, a harmony, between himself and them that would strengthen all of them.

As Azurebella's people were submerged in the peaceful waters and the story ended, he felt relaxed and refreshed, hopeful about resolving his problem. He noticed that he felt much better than he had before the story and music began.

Another man, the manager of a theater, found himself face to face with the issue of the abandonment he had experienced in his life. Identifying with the abandoned baby dragon, he re-experienced being abandoned at three years of age when his parents had divorced.

The man had been happily married for fifteen years and knew he loved his wife, but recently had been dreaming of an old girlfriend he had loved. Years ago, she had left him, without warning, and had married someone else. He needed to find out why she had done this. His dreams had disturbed him and left him wondering if he had married the wrong woman. Yet he had been reluctant to look up his old girlfriend even though he knew where she lived, for fear it might destroy his marriage.

During the *Riversea Goddess* story, he experienced some powerful feeling images. He saw himself meeting with his former love and sharing his feelings with her. Then he saw himself with his wife and felt that nothing could come between them. It was a much-needed rehearsal. The message, which led to new insight, was clear: it was vital to his well-being to get some closure with his old girlfriend. He knew now that his marriage would remain secure.

Though deep unconscious thoughts and feelings are often brought to consciousness with the story, which is designed to stimulate the senses and emotions, and the music, which itself contains powerful moments of tension and resolution, there have been instances where people focus on the music, and the story becomes deeply submerged in their unconscious. Even though they have no conscious memory of the story, it remains in their unconscious until such time as they are ready to deal with the issues it evokes within them.

In one series of individual GIM sessions, my client was a teacher who had taken a class with me four months earlier in which I had read the *Riversea Goddess* story. In one particular GIM session, she became very relaxed and began talking about the images she was seeing in her mind's eye.

She was seeing a vast ocean, and emerging from that ocean was a baby dragon. The dragon was slimy and covered with mud and gunk from the bottom of the ocean. It told her it was looking for its mother. Slimy though it was, she befriended it and helped it find its mother.

After the session was over, I remarked how interesting it was that she should have imaged that dragon from the *Riversea Goddess* story. My client said, "What dragon? I remember Azurebella and that peaceful kingdom, but I don't remember any dragon!" Apparently, what that dragon had represented in her consciousness was too threatening at the time, and she had absorbed it at a deeper level to be dealt with when she felt safe to do so.

Music and Normal and "Disturbed" Children

Other experiences with the results of the *Riversea Goddess* story shook the very foundation of my logical mind. They led me to wonder if children in mental hospitals were emotionally healthier and more creative than children in regular public schools.

When I first began documenting the effects of my therapeutic metaphorical stories, I visited a number of elementary and middle schools. After listening to the story and music, the children were asked to draw the images, colors, feelings, sounds and even tastes and smells the story to music brought to them.

Some children connected with the beauty and harmony of the natural universe, and their drawings reflected that beauty and sense of wholeness. Most children had more difficulty shutting out the exterior world even for a few moments. Perhaps they were afraid of the feelings that were brewing in their inner selves — feelings they had never been encouraged to acknowledge.

These children, unaccustomed to their own unique feelings and creative thoughts, were the ones who copied their neighbors' drawings. Many of the pictures were very ordinary drawings of houses and trees and showed little creativity or originality. The children drew what they felt was expected of them rather than tapping into their own inner wisdom. My sense is that they had wonderful, colorful imagery with the music, but had learned how to shut it off because it might be considered "weird" or different.

At the same time, I began to wonder if my stories were lacking in evocative power. Then I visited a mental hospital and read the *Riversea Goddess* to a group of "disturbed" adolescents.

Below are three examples of the different responses which the story generated. The first is a charming fairy tale-like illustration showing Azurebella and the dragon, who is floating in on a raft. The chaos is conveyed by a black line of clouds and flashes of lightning.

The next drawing illustrates the harmony and unity that this young man felt while listening to the music and story. Despite the beauty of the tree, notice that the lowest limb has been cut off. The tree, like the young man, is not whole.

A 16-year-old girl there drew the third picture. I was fascinated by the images and symbols she had drawn out of the depth of her being. I asked her to write about the picture, and this is what she wrote:

> *Because Azurebella is half divine, she has no real body formation when you first look at her. Her person is that of a mystic goblet, for she soaks up everything in her surroundings. You can see forever in her eyes, as well as the sea, which for her represents sanctuary, for everything is serene as she bathes within the holy waters, and peace is prevalent within the air until the creature breathes his fire and causes the wisdom in the goblet to spill over and onto the earth. And when it hits the atmosphere, others can now appreciate her beauty.*

I was taken aback. This young girl, labeled "emotionally disturbed," had brought forth, from the deep unconscious, profound archetypes, or universal symbols, such as the goblet, the star and crescent moon symbol, the ankh symbol, and fire. In her description of the drawing, she expressed the Jungian concept of the shadow: that we must deal with the dark, sometimes frightening, aspects of ourselves and integrate them before we can truly appreciate our own beauty and self-worth.

I asked this sensitive young girl if she knew anything about Carl Jung and his work. She did not. Neither did she consciously understand the significance of the archetypal symbols she drew. But unconsciously she understood. This girl, as well as other young people in the group, were accustomed to dealing with their feelings every day; talking about them, acknowledging them, and honoring the world inside them.

As I left the mental hospital, I asked myself who was mentally healthier: these "maladjusted" young people or the thousands of photocopied children in our public schools and mass-produced adults in our corporate world who seem "well adjusted," yet are cut off from their inner essence because they may not know it exists.

Music Activity #16
Music for Waking and Sleeping

I suggest the following pieces of music to wake you in the morning, energize you, and get you ready for the day:

Giuliani	*Guitar Concertos*
Grieg	*Peer Gynt Suite*—also called *Morning Mood*
Haydn	*The String Quartets*
Mozart	*Piano Concertos*
Telemann	*Flute Concertos*
Vivaldi	*The Four Seasons*

The following pieces of music are calming and quieting, and may help you fall asleep, and sleep well:

Bach	*Air on a G string*
Bach	*Sonata No. 4 for Flute & Harpsichord—"Siciliano"*
Debussy	*Claire de Lune*
Haydn	*Cello Concerto in C Major (second movement)*
Mozart	*Flute and Harp Concerto, (second movement)*
Pachelbel	*Canon in D*

Notes

1. Assagioli, Roberto, *Psychosynthesis*. Penguin Books (New York), 1976, p. 240.

2. McClellan, *The Healing Forces of Music*. Amity House (Amity, New York), 1988, p. 38.

3. Zukav, Gary, *The Dancing Wu Li Masters*. Bantam Books (New York), 1979, p. xxvii.

4. McClellan, Randall, *The Healing Forces of Music*. Amity House (Amity, New York), 1988, p. 127.

5. Zukav, Gary, *The Dancing Wu Li Masters*. Bantam Books (New York), 1979, p. 313.

6. Swimme, Brian, "Do-re-mi and the Galaxy." *Creation*, July/August 1986, Vol. 2 No. 3, p. 25.

7. McClellan, Randall, *The Healing Forces of Music*. Amity House (Amity, New York), 1988, p. 121-122.

8. Swimme, Brian, "Do-re-mi and the Galaxy." *Creation*, July/August 1986, Vol. 2 No. 3, p. 25.

9. Lingerman, Hal, *The Healing Energies of Music*. The Theosophical Publishing House (Wheaton, IL), 1983, p. 63, 67.

Body, Mind, Spirit and Music

*"What song did the great fireball sing? What tune accompanied the forma-
tion of the galaxies? The music that ushered in the cosmos plays on, inside
us and around us."*

-Brian Swimme

Thanks to educators like Lozanov, we are beginning to notice that
our heads are actually connected to our bodies. Our bodies, too, can
learn. On the other hand, if our bodies are stressed, anxious or exhausted,
they can make the neurons in our brains backfire, so that we are either
not thinking clearly or not thinking at all.

If our souls are untouched or uninspired, only part of our brain is in
gear. When we learn with our whole being, we can tap into the mental
reserves that contain our full potential. Lozanov included ethical, moral
and spiritual enhancement as important components of the music to be
used for successful development. If the music helps you think more clearly and relax your body but does not inspire you to reach higher or help

you attain your own nobility, spirituality and strength, then it does not succeed in activating your potential.

Learning, insight and creative problem-solving can be stimulated by the language of imagery integrated with great music. The music alone, without story, also has great capacity to connect with our deeper selves. Here the range of response of body, brain/mind and spirit is even wider since the consciousness is freer to let the music carry it wherever it wants to go. It can deal with conflict if it chooses, or awaken deep spiritual awareness. On a lighter level, it can guide us into exploring a new idea for an advertising campaign or take us for a walk on the beach.

When exploring the effects of both Music Imaging and story with music, it is instructive to notice the changes music can create in the body, brain, emotions and spirit so that these responses may be brought to a conscious level. In this way, we can learn how to use music in our lives for personal and spiritual transformation, as well as tapping the unused capacity of our brains. We can learn to honor the mysterious power of music even though we may not understand exactly how it works.

How Music Alters Physiological Functions

In the world we live in, it is easy to lose touch with the natural, slow rhythms of life. In an effort to achieve the ideals of a material, goal-oriented society, we speed up the pace of our lives to the point where we are out of sync with the steady primal earthbeat.

When we learn to experience music as therapy, these tendencies can be counteracted and even reversed. We can feel the music nourishing us, and putting us back in touch with the primal roots of our being. When I ask people how their bodies feel with a certain piece of music, they often use words like "wonderful!" "refreshed!" "relaxed!" or "energetic!" When we become aware of how music alters particular physiological functions in our bodies, many people begin to notice changes in their pulse rates, their muscle strength or their circulation. Rhythm, a major element of music, is a primal force in our lives. In fact, the very first thing we experience in utero is our mother's heartbeat.

When resonators are close to each other and their energies interact, there is a tendency for the resonators to come into sync with each other and resonate at the same frequency. The pendulums of two clocks ticking slightly offbeat from each other will begin to synchronize when placed in close proximity. This simple yet intriguing fact has powerful implications for our potential to control the influences in our environment.

Using Music to Stimulate or Calm Yourself

This phenomenon is called *entrainment,* and it explains why our heartbeat tends to synchronize with the beat of the music we listen to. In a famous experiment conducted in a baby nursery, Lee Salk conducted an experiment playing heartbeat sounds to the newborns, while keeping track of their food intake and weight gain. One group of babies heard the broadcast of heartbeats at the normal rate of 72 beats per minute, while others heard no heartbeats. Though they ate the same amount of food, 70 percent of the babies that heard the heartbeat gained more weight than those who did not. When Salk tried broadcasting an abnormally fast heartbeat (128 beats per minute), the babies got so upset that he couldn't finish that part of the experiment; they may have perceived the quickened beat as a flashback to some nervous experience of the pregnant mothers.1

Entrainment works the same way when it comes to the music we listen to. If the tempo of the music gets faster, our hearts will beat faster. Since the human heart beats, at normal activity, at somewhere between 70 and 80 beats per minute, a tempo faster than this can stimulate you or raise your tension level.

If you want to calm down, you would use music with a slower tempo. *Largo* or *Adagio* are names given to the slow movements of larger works of Baroque music by composers such as Bach, Handel, Vivaldi and Corelli. These slow movements have a tempo of 60 beats per minute, and thus have a calming, relaxing effect. Slow movements of some Classical and Romantic pieces can also slow down organic rhythms. If you are feeling tense, you might want to first match your tense mood and gradually work into music with a slower tempo.

The *iso principle* (short for "isomorphic," Greek for "same form"), an offshoot of entrainment, is about matching your music to your mood. If you come home from work after a stressful day and you're feeling tense and emotionally drained, you might not want to listen to a light, airy Mozart flute sonata. Instead, you might choose a more serene piece of music; one that would resonate with your mood, such as the *Adagio* by Albinoni, the *Pachelbel Canon in D,* or even the slow movement of the *Haydn Cello Concerto.* As the music helps you release your tension and moves you to a new place emotionally, you could then switch to a lighter, more energetic type of music.

The ebb and flow of our breathing also adjusts itself to the sounds around us. We can slow it down or speed it up with music. The first theme from the Brahms' *Fourth Symphony (first movement)* breathes at a more or less regular rate of respiration. After listening to the first ten seconds of this selection participants at my workshops notice an appreciable drop in their respiration rate.

Chaotic music with irregular rhythms can speed up our heart rate and actually change its rhythm. Music with an irregular rhythm can also be disturbing to the body by causing an irregular heart rhythm. Not only are our hearts affected by the rhythms around us, but our muscular movements are affected, as well as the subtle rhythms of every cell, molecule and atom in our bodies. Music can stimulate or calm them, balance them, or jar and disrupt them.

According to *American Health* magazine, Jacqueline Sue Chapman discovered that premature babies gained more weight and became healthier with Brahms Lullaby. For her doctoral dissertation at N.Y.U., Chapman studied 153 premature infants in three hospitals. The group that had the Brahms recording piped in beneath their incubators six times daily were discharged an average of one week before the babies who did not listen to the lullaby. Because the music soothed the babies, it reduced the number of extraneous movements, conserving energy desperately needed for survival.[2]

Dr. Thomas Verny, author of *The Secret Life of the Unborn Child,* informs us that many musicians, including Artur Rubinstein and Yehudi Menuhin, claim that they became interested in music while they were still in the womb.[3] A friend of mine, who made a cassette tape of Adagio (slow), movements for his pregnant wife, thinks it probably piqued his children's musical interest even before they came into this world. At four and a half, while watching a TV broadcast of Beethoven's *Ninth Symphony,* his son conducted the entire symphony along with Leonard Bernstein! This same friend has a colleague who has a passion for Rachmaninoff. He claims Rachmaninoff was his mother's favorite composer, and that she played it all the time she was pregnant with him.

Music and Your Muscles

Music also enables athletes and exercisers to do strenuous exercise without suffering undue strain. At Ohio State University, Gopi A. Tejwani and other researchers have found that music lowers the psychological stress of exercise. Aside from making exercise more pleasant, allowing you to stay with your exercise program, it keeps you from getting tired and enables you to push harder with less effort. It also regulates your breathing and promotes better muscle coordination. In one of their studies, it was found that men who ran on a treadmill while listening to upbeat music such as Diana Ross and Michael Jackson, felt less tired and had significantly lower amounts of beta-endorphin, a natural opiate the brain releases when it reacts to pain or stress.[4] It might be interesting to test some upbeat classical music such as Mozart or Haydn and compare results.

In a study at Stanford University Medical Center, scientists measured muscle activity as 24 women aged 18 to 35 put pegs inside holes, to the accompaniment of both even and uneven musical rhythms. The group exposed to even rhythms was able to accomplish their task significantly faster than the group that labored under the uneven beat.[5]

According to Dr. John Diamond, your body can actually determine which music is beneficial to your health and which is detrimental. Diamond's predecessor, Dr. George Goodheart, discovered that each major muscle of the body is related to an organ, so that a weakness in a particular muscle can indicate energy depletion in the related organ. Working on the hypothesis that our overall energy level is manifested in our muscle strength and can be influenced by environment and lifestyle, Diamond tested the response of hundreds of people to different pieces of music over several years' time.

The method he used is simple but effective. The test subject is asked to extend her or his arm straight out to the side of her or his body. The tester then pushes down on the extended arm just above the wrist. This tests the strength of the middle deltoid muscle. Since many muscles of the body relate to an organ, this implies that our organs are being affected as well. Diamond discovered that when test subjects listen to music during the tests, their muscular strength varies widely. Certain pieces of music result in pronounced muscle weakening; others result in the test subject testing stronger than before. Diamond tested over 20,000 recordings of all types of music. Only two pieces of classical music produced muscle weakness: Stravinsky's *Rite of Spring* and Ravel's *La Valse*.[6]

As well as the music to which we expose ourselves, Diamond believes that various influences in our environment and life-style are constantly affecting our life energy. He tells us that:

> *Many of the factors that lower energy are products of the technological revolution: the poisons and noises in our environment, the overrefined and unnatural foods we find on the supermarket shelves, the synthetic fabrics from which so many of our clothes are made.*[7]

Music or Aspirin?

Music is being used more and more as a painkiller. Psychologist Janet Lapp of California State University found that music used with imagery and relaxation techniques reduced the number, intensity and duration of migraine headaches. For migraines that are caused by tension, Lapp believes music is one of the best ways to induce relaxation and relieve the headache. She used relaxation training combined with either biofeedback or music. She offered two thirty minute sessions a week for five weeks.

After keeping track of their headaches during the training, and for more than a year after the training, the music group had the best results. They had only one-sixth as many headaches as they had had previously, and their headaches were milder and of shorter duration. Music helped to dissolve a headache before it took hold. Lapp found music easier to utilize than biofeedback, since it does not require cumbersome equipment. She commented that music may induce relaxation so well because it releases endorphins, the body's natural painkillers.[8]

In Poland, an experimental group of patients with severe headaches and neurological disorders listened to symphonic music for six months. The findings revealed that they required much less medication and painkillers than the rest of the 408 patients tested.[9]

"Prescribing" Music

If music can strengthen or weaken your muscles, slow down or speed up your breathing, decrease or increase your heart rate, and integrate your brain, why haven't we used it more consciously? It seems odd to imagine a doctor prescribing a Bach concerto or a Beethoven sonata, but music as medicine often works as well as caffeine or tranquilizers, and there are no side effects! According to Lozanov, in the future we will be able to isolate the various influences within each piece of music and determine its effect on every individual at a given moment.[15] Perhaps music will be prescribed for such maladies as tension, depression, lethargy, high blood pressure, and many other disorders.

A friend of mine uses music every time his back goes out. The soothing strains relax the muscle tension in his body. When he wants to relieve
the tension in his body, he does his own body work to music. He retires
to a very private corner of his home and turns the lights down very low.
Then he turns on either a Strauss waltz such as Tales from the Vienna
Woods or *On The Beautiful Blue Danube,* or he might choose some quiet
guitar music or the romantic symphonies of Tchaikovsky or Brahms. He
dances freestyle to the music, or does yoga, or uses a back roller up and
down his back. The music provides the emotional exercise and feels nurturing and comforting. It helps dissipate his tension, and when he
emerges from his dimly-lit, private corner, his back feels much better.

There are now about 5,000 music therapists using music in treatment
programs all over the United States. Music therapist Jayne Standley of
Florida State University claims that stress during and after surgery has
been reduced with music. She found that patients who heard music while
under anesthesia had lower levels of the stress-related hormones cortisol
and noradrenaline than those who did not. In another study she did,
patients who listened to music during the 48 hours following surgery
were found to have lower blood pressure and pulse rates than those who
did not take doses of music.[10]

Dr. Helen Bonny found that heart patients who listened to the
"Music Rx" tapes that she developed had less pain and anxiety as well as
lower blood pressure and pulse rates.[11]

She tested her tapes first at Jefferson Hospital in Port Townsend,
Washington, where the hospital staff monitored the vital signs of patients
before and after they listened to the specially selected music. According to
Carolyn Latteier in an article from *Medical Self-Care,* the staff also rated
the patients' emotional states using the Emotional Condition Rating
Scale. This is a widely used measure of emotional experience which
arranges emotions on a continuum from negative (fear, anxiety, hate, etc.)
to positive (security, well-being, love, etc.). In addition, doctors and nurs-

es were asked to report how they felt their patients responded to the tapes.

After listening to the music, patients' heart rates and blood pressure lowered, and there were significant changes from negative to positive on the Emotional Rating Scale. Also, patients did not require as much pain medication. A nurse at the hospital commented:

> *Pain is more than a physical sensation. It's a mind/body experience that also involves anxiety. People's level of anxiety has a great deal to do with how they perceive their pain. The music helped reduce their anxiety. As a result, they felt less pain and had less need for pain medication.* [12]

Bonny 's tapes were also played during and after surgery. Not only were pain and anxiety reduced, but half the amount of anesthesia was necessary.[13] The patients were not the only ones who were less anxious. According to Latteier, the doctors and nurses loved the music too. "Several staff members reported decreased job anxiety, increased tolerance of patient demands, and improved job satisfaction in general." "Music Rx" is now used in 40 other hospitals.

Bonny herself found that she could heal her own damaged heart through classical music. When she was in her mid-fifties and very active as director of the Music Therapy Department at Catholic University in Baltimore, during which time she also maintained a private practice, ran the Institute for Consciousness and Music, played the violin in an orchestra, and managed a family, she was suddenly struck down by an attack of severe angina.

She was told that she would have to completely change her lifestyle. For a long time, she led a sedentary life. But she felt frustrated and depressed at having to curtail her activities. One day, she made a conscious decision that she was not willing to accept the verdict of a passive existence as her fate.

She decided to get well. Using music, and meditating on her body cells, she recovered in body and spirit.

At the University of Massachusetts Medical Center in Worcester, Jon Kabat-Zinn, director of the stress reduction and relaxation program, takes patients through a meditation based on Buddhist teachings. Patients learn how to become aware of their breathing patterns, and how their positive or negative thoughts are affecting their health. Harpist Georgia Kelley provides background music for the program.

Instead of tranquilizers, some doctors are now prescribing Kabat-Zinn's program to help patients cope with the anxiety of being hospitalized, and as a tool to handle pain that wakes them during the night. According to an article in *New Age Journal*:

> *Understanding pain and how it can be relieved has been a major concern of modern medicine for some time, and researchers are now experimenting with alternative therapies such as music, guided visualization, hypnosis, and meditation to treat pain as a total experience. Perhaps the most complicated dimension of being sick, the pain of experience is a constellation of side-effects that include physical tension, emotional distress and depression, loss of communication skills, a disordered sense of time, and a limited range of mobility. Researchers have found that effecting change in any one of those areas can profoundly transform the patient's self-image and world-view, and consequently, the experience of the pain itself.*[14]

Pain and disease often have an emotional root cause. Working with music, imagery and the emotions can help prevent or ameliorate many types of physical ills.

As more is discovered about the neurotransmitters in the brain and the cells' response to vibration, more specific musical remedies may be developed. So-called "incurable" illness may be treated and healed. Music as a preventive measure, moreover, has vast possibilities. We know now that much illness is caused by emotional trauma, stress, worry and pent-up feelings. Many people with high blood pressure and other stress-related diseases have learned to meditate. They have learned to open themselves up to a more expansive state of mind where they can be still. Music alone can bring you to that state of mind. Music combined with meditation helps you move into that place of stillness even more easily.

Life Streams, a new book by Hal A. Lingerman, offers a meditation for every day of the year, with accompanying musical selections.

Music Activity #17
Exercising to Music

Try playing the five pieces mentioned in Chapter 1 to do different kinds of exercise.

- With the *Pachelbel Canon in D* you can do T'ai Chi or slow dance movements. Let the music bring you an image; perhaps a fern-filled glade or a grassy meadow. Dance the images.
- With the *Four Seasons* by Vivaldi, try fast walking and see if you have more endurance. *The Bach Brandenburg Concertos* would also be suitable for walking.
- You could run to *Eine Kleine Nachtmusik* by Mozart. This piece is also suitable for low impact aerobics or stretching exercises.
- If you have your own swimming pool, try using *Prelude to the Afternoon of a Faun* by Debussy for graceful movement in the water.
- As an experiment, compare exercising to music by Michael Jackson or other rock stars. Notice how you feel, not just during the exercise, but afterwards, as well.

Music Activity #18
Music to Calm You

The following table gives particular movements of different pieces that have rhythms of 65 beats per minute or less. Many people have found it useful to make a tape of just these slow movements of each piece, leaving out the other movements. The tape can then be played at those times when you wish to get back in touch with your slow natural rhythms. When making your selections it is important to remember that each person responds differently to a given piece. You should test your own personal responses using the techniques above, and in previous chapters, before choosing your music for relaxation.

Bach, J.S.	Concerto for Two Violins in D minor (second movement)
	Arioso from Cantata No. 156
	Sarabande, Bouree from Violin Partita, No. 1
Beethoven	Piano Concerto No. 5, "Emperor" (second movement)
	Violin Concerto (second movement)
Brahms	Symphony No. 3 (second movement)
Grieg	*Holberg Suite, Air*
Haydn	Cello Concerto (second movement)
Mozart	Concerto for Flute and Harp (second movement)
	Piano Concerto No. 21 (second movement)
Prokofiev	Symphony No. 5 (second movement)
Schubert	Unfinished Symphony (second movement)
Tchaikovsky	Symphony No. 6 (second movement)

Music Activity #19
Music to Stimulate You

The following table is a selection of movements, taken from longer pieces, that have a fast, up-beat rhythm of 80 beats or more, from which you can select a number that stimulate you without causing stress. As with calming music, you could make a tape consisting of just these movements, out of the context of the larger pieces from which they are taken. This tape would be useful at times when you need to be energized: days when you have a hard time waking up; afternoons when you are dragging; after work before a big date, and so on. It is as always important to be in tune with your body and get its opinion on what the effects of each movement really are: a piece that energizes one person may stress another. Use the exercises above to determine your body's response before you make up your "pick-me-up" tape.

J.S. Bach	Brandenburg Concerto Nos. 2 and 4 (first movement)
	Concerto for Two Violins in D Minor (first movement)

Beethoven   Symphony No. 3, "Eroica" (fourth movement)

Piano Concerto No. 5, "Emperor" (first and/or third movement)

Waldstein Piano Sonata (first movement)

Brahms   Symphony No. 2 (last movement)

Glinka   Overture to *Ruslan and Ludmilla*

Haydn   Symphony No. 98 (first movement)

Mendelssohn   Violin Concerto (first movement)

Italian Symphony (fourth movement)

Mozart   *Eine Kleine Machtmusik*

Piano Concerto No. 21 (first movement)

Rodrigo   *Concierto de Aranjuez* (first movement)

Smetana   Overture to *The Bartered Bride*

Verdi   Triumphal March from *Aida*

Vivaldi   Concerto for Two Trumpets in C major (last movement)

Notes

1. Ingber, Dina, Brody, Robert, and Pearson, Cliff, "Music Therapy: Tune-up for Mind and Body." *Science Digest,* January 1982, p. 78.

2. Wein, Bibi, "Body and Soul Music," *American Health,* April 1987, p. 70.

3. Verny, Thomas, with Kelly, John, *The Secret Life of the Unborn Child.* Dell (New York), 1981, p. 39.

4. Brody, Robert, "Winning Combo: Muscle and Music." *Los Angeles Times,* April 9, 1988, Part V, p. 4

5. Ibid.

6. Diamond, John, *Your Body Doesn't Lie.* Warner Books (New York), 1980, p. 163.

7. Ibid., p. 33, 34.

8. Chance, Paul, "Music Hath Charms to Soothe a Throbbing Head." *Psychology Today,* February 1987, p. 14.

9. Ingber, Dina, Brody, Robert, and Pearson, Cliff, "Music Therapy: Tune-up for Mind and Body." *Science Digest,* January 1982, p. 78.

10. Wein, Bibi, "Body and Soul Music." *American Health*, April, 1987, p. 70-71.

11. *Music Rx* tapes are available from: The Bonny Foundation, 2020 Simmons Street, Salinas, KS 67401.

12. Latteier, Carolyn, "Music as Medicine." *Medical Self-Care,* November/December 1985, p.51.

13. Ibid., p. 51.

14. Bloom, Pamela, "Soul Music," *New Age Journal,* March/April 1987, p. 60.

The Rhythm of Emotion

Music is the shorthand of emotion. Emotions which let themselves be described in words with such difficulty are directly conveyed to man in music, and in that is its power and significance.

—Leo Tolstoy

Rhythmic patterns and melodic shape, harmony and timbre, all reach our emotions. They communicate to us in a subconscious language that has a much greater impact than mere words. Composer Aaron Copland called music "a vast language without a dictionary, whose symbols are interpreted by the listener according to some unwritten Esperanto of the emotions." Esperanto is an international language of words; music is a universal language of the emotions.

As you listen to a piece of music, you directly receive the message it brings to you alone at that moment. Perhaps the slow, or Largo, movement of a Bach violin concerto might evoke the remembrance of yourself as a young parent, holding your baby. The baby is now grown up and on his or her own, living a life you can only glimpse, but the strains of the music revive the feeling of his warm little body against yours, his sweet talcum scent, eager eyes and expectant smile. You re-experience the joy of being a new parent. Another person, listening to the same selection, might find it releases her or his grief over the loss of a relative. Still another might become deeply immersed in a transpersonal experience.

On one of his compositions, Beethoven wrote, "From the heart may it find its way to the heart." He did not say "head" because hearing music with only your rational faculties is not really hearing what the composer has to say. Just as Beethoven, deaf in his later years, could feel his music without physically hearing it, so can we experience music's impact on our emotions without explaining it.

Music can do things to our emotions that defy analysis or understanding. The language of the heart reaches areas of the brain, such as the right hemisphere of the cerebral cortex, or the limbic system, which do not respond to purely intellectual communication. Music involves the heart in the learning process. Great music comes from the heart of the composer, not just from his mind.

One of the most powerful aspects of music is its wholeness and its ability to evoke a total response within us. When we listen to a piece of music, we respond holistically. Our bodies do not respond without something changing in our emotions. Our emotions can alter our bodily functions. Our thinking processes are affected by how our bodies feel. All of these, in turn, affect our spirit; whether it feels uplifted or despondent, attuned to God, or remote from Him. Music engages all the layers of the brain and personality at once. The patterns in the music stimulate emotional patterns on different levels simultaneously. As we hear the tension and release in the music, it reminds us of different physical, emotional and mental responses that have the same energy pattern.

Imagine a kaleidoscope with many different patterns arranged within one large pattern. Imagine that each pattern represents a different part of us: our physical being, our emotional nature, our intellectual and our spiritual aspects. Imagine that the music is the mover. If the music were to turn the kaleidoscope, all of the smaller patterns might shift at once, not just one or two of them. A simultaneous shifting of the whole is powerful enough to not only change our mood, but to unleash transformative energies within the psyche. Music, always in constant movement, shifts and changes, and we, as resonators, shift and change along with it.

Ultimately, our very souls open up as a result of all of these things happening simultaneously, as music enables us to go through the veils that separate us from the Self. Scientists in past ages, as well as spiritual leaders of today, have claimed that beyond altering our moods and state of mind, music can bring us back to our true essence.

Aristotle spoke of rhythm and melody as evoking such qualities as gentleness and courage. Dissonant, chaotic music, on the other hand, can often isolate us from our souls, leading us to take on aggressive and belligerent characteristics. During World War II, Hitler used some of Richard Wagner's music to arouse aggressive feelings in his soldiers. Wagner had a very erratic personality that fluctuated between the narcissistic and the inspired. Other music by him could inspire the soul.

A composer cannot write into music any value or point of view that is not part of his own personality. When we hear the music, those values are transmitted to us subconsciously. Mozart's powers of intuition, for example, were very strong, and he wrote those intuitive elements into his music. When you listen to Mozart, you get in touch with your own intuitive powers. According to Manfred Clynes, who has done extensive research into the psychoneurology of music, when you listen to a piece of great music the inner essence of the composer, or what he calls the musical pulse, is revealed to you. You can know his essence and his nature. That pulse contains his way of looking at the world.

For instance, the pulse of Beethoven has a more ego-involved, Dionysian character than Mozart, whose point of view is more serene and detached. This is detected subconsciously by the listener through the manner in which a musical phrase is repeated. Each composer repeats phrases slightly differently. As minute as these differences might be, they can cause great differences in spiritual meaning. As we become more aware of these subconscious influences, we become able to use music to develop various aspects of ourselves.

Freeing Your Inner Rhythms

When we think of the effect of rhythm upon us, we think of the rhythms of the body, but our emotions have their rhythms as well. Psychologist Roberto Assagioli believes that music can be the cause of disease or a catalyst for healing. Our emotional rhythms–depression and elation, sorrow and joy, strength and weakness–are highly influenced by the rhythm of the music we hear. Through the tension and release in the music, expectations are set up as to what the music might do next. These expectations may be frustrated or fulfilled. As we listen, we feel that frustration or fulfillment.

If we were to acknowledge the rhythm of our emotions; if it were acceptable in our culture to feel them and let others see us expressing them, we could let them breathe vitality into us as they were meant to do. Then our emotions could keep us healthy and well-balanced.

It has been found that the members of one particular profession live much longer than the average person. Even in their seventies and eighties they are healthy and well-balanced. They usually have tremendous energy and vitality. Who are these people who grow in world esteem at ages when most of us have long been retired; who continue to refine their art and give pleasure to thousands, sometimes millions, of people, and whose work is cherished and collected long after they have left this life? Their names are Arturo Toscanini, Leopold Stokowski, Pierre Monteux, Leonard Bernstein, Georg Solti, and many others—all conductors of large orchestras.

Besides pleasure in their work, what keeps these men functioning at the highest level of their powers well into old age? The ever-energetic Bernstein was in his seventies and von Karajan was over eighty when he died! The answer has much to do with the simple physical actions involved in conducting. Most of us hold our tension in our necks and shoulders. Conductors, leading their orchestras, constantly move their arms above their heads, releasing the tightness in their necks and shoulders and exercising their heart muscles.

This is among the best forms of aerobic exercise possible. The circulation and metabolism of these conductors get greater stimulation than with any other kind of exercise. At the same time, they are taking in the full, rich sounds and vibrations of the music throughout their whole being. Since many of the gestures we make express the body's response to an imbalance in our energy system, conductors' movements are expressing the hundreds of emotions they are subconsciously feeling, thus balancing their energy systems. It is no wonder that their energy carries them through old age and that, despite their years, they remain young.

Balancing Body, Soul and Spirit

When we learn to spend as much time exercising our emotions as we do exercising our bodies, we, too, will become healthier and more balanced. We can all live a fuller emotional life.

Recently, scientists have been making spectacular discoveries about the nature of emotion. Dr. Manfred Clynes has developed the science of sentics–the study of the communication of the emotions. He has isolated what he calls "essentic forms" for seven basic emotions: Love, Hate, Reverence, Grief, Anger, Joy, and Sex. At the beginning of life, each emotion is neurologically coded into the brain, and corresponds to, and can be triggered by, a specific pattern. Clynes has tested experimental subjects by having them feel a particular emotion while resting their finger on a device which measures pressure. When the intensity of this pressure is plotted on a graph, the patterns correspond to similar emotions evoked by pieces of music. Conversely, music which expresses a particular emotion activates its corresponding essentic form in the brain. The patterns are strikingly uniform across cultures and the sexes.

Music communicates through essentic form:

Traditionally, the question of how music communicates—how it changes our states and gives us insights—has mainly been the concern of aesthetics or of music criticism. But we may regard the language of music also scientifically, in the perspective of the existence of essentic forms. A good composer who intends a particular portion of music to communicate joy can do just that. The performer who understands the composer's intention can induce joy, and a listener can be sensitive to the performance and perceive joy, a reflection of the vision of joy the composer created perhaps hundreds of years before—all this is possible through the function and stability of essentic form.[1]

Essentic forms are the elements of music just as letters are the elements of language. The more purely a performer reproduces the essentic form, the greater the effect of the music to reflect and express emotion . As we listen to great performers, we know intuitively that they have captured the pulse of the composer. We feel moved by the music. It touches us very deeply and inspires us in ways that words cannot express.

Emotions can also be exercised (and generated) by a procedure Clynes developed called *sentic cycles.* Finger pressure on a finger rest is used in a specific way to express an emotional state. This is done for a number of different emotions until the sentic cycle is completed. Using a computer, as mentioned above, the pattern of the finger pressure can be converted into a visual representation on a graph, and even into sound. Practicing the expressing of emotions opens up many locked-up aspects of the person. Dr. Clynes' subjects, as they work regularly with sentic cycles, feel more relaxed, healthy, and at peace with themselves.

Clynes found that:

The emotional state acts as a focus to draw memories, associations and thoughts into the consciousness of the performer of sentic cycles. Thus in addition to the neurochemical effect that the generation of emotion itself may have on the organism…effects are also released which may relate to specific memories, catharsis and spontaneously generated creative ideas.[2]

Other research on releasing emotions has questioned whether or not it is healthy to habitually express anger, as it has been found to lead to more frequent and intense bouts of anger. Experience with Guided Imagery and Music suggests to me that allowing yourself to connect with your anger or rage and experiencing it in an altered state of consciousness releases it much more effectively and safely than practicing your anger on your friends.

We can practice expressing our emotions in a generalized way without directing them at a particular person. Listening to an inspired piece of music or experiencing sentic cycles are safe ways to generate an emotion, release it, and move on to the next one. As I listen to music, I often feel anger or sadness being released even when I have not consciously connected that feeling to anyone or anything in particular. In working with Dr. Clynes on sentic cycles, I noticed that even though I was expressing anger using finger pressure, I had no particular associations connected to that anger. I just felt it.

At the *Music in Medicine* symposium in West Germany in 1984, Clynes reported that most probably there are specific neurochemicals for each basic emotion and that the emotional exercise and release experienced with music can increase the activity of the immune system. The effects of auditory stimuli, stress, and other environmental factors on the body's immune system have been noted, and experiments bearing out these effects compiled, by researcher Robert Ader at the University of Rochester.[3] Clynes notes that the death rate of musicians from cancer is quite a bit lower than for the population as a whole. Clynes believes that essentic forms bridge the gap between the heart, the mind, and the body, and that crossing the bridge leads to new avenues of healing.

Music, Learning and Our Emotions

We learn best when we are free to express ourselves. Yet our society does everything it can to discourage that free expression. It is embarrassing to cry or get angry in front of others. It is considered unacceptable to shout and jump up and down for joy. We have learned to bury our feelings, and we have learned it well. Since our culture makes it unacceptable for us to recognize and honor feelings of anger, depression, jealousy or grief, we swallow them as soon as they well up inside us. Later, we notice a lump in our throats or a constriction in our chests, or we develop thyroid problems or suffer anxiety or depression.

As teachers and parents, we can help our children open up to the life-long process of joyful learning by giving them permission to feel. Rather than telling our children or loved ones not to cry, we would be more help letting them know it is alright to be sad, and supporting them through it.

Rather than being fearful of their anger and telling them, "Don't be angry!" we might encourage them to express their anger right then, when they are feeling it, as long as they don't hurt anyone. If they do not air that anger in the moment, it may express itself in destructive, insidious ways later on. If we become accustomed to expressing our emotions via sentic cycles or other positive methods, we need not endanger others either physically or verbally. Emotions can and should be expressed in a tempered way, whether alone or to others, so that they don't come rushing out in one great big torrent at a later time.

Our own attitudes about feelings are crucial to the development of feelings of those around us, and we cannot help them if we have not learned how to handle our own feelings. Helen Bonny has this to say about GIM and emotional expression:

> *In our culture the opposite stance is taken, where feelings are not allowed open expression except in certain ritual situations such as funerals, weddings, films, sports events, etc. A person's emotional nature, as a result, is stifled. Not only are negative emotions suppressed, i.e., those which create illnesses of body and spirit, but beautiful feelings are stifled as well. The spirit cannot become full, the body cannot become radiantly healthy, without the experience of beauty found in the fullest use of the senses.* [4]

According to Bonny, it is possible to discover what is causing free-floating anxiety, and to work out anger and hostility, in the safe context of music.

What is the connection between learning and the emotions? It is a process we are just beginning to understand. Much has been discovered recently about how the emotions stimulate the brain to enhance learning. Emotions such as nostalgia or excitement can stimulate the connections of neurons in the brain. Feelings and information flow together in new ways, bringing creative connections.

At first, the emotional influences take the form of subconscious impressions on the periphery of your attention. At a later time, they may activate a certain memory and bring it into your consciousness. Just as emotion has the capability of stimulating learning and memory, bottled-up emotions can obscure thoughts, block memory, stifle creativity and stunt personal and spiritual growth. We will consider this further in Chapter 8, Music and the Multiple Brain/Mind. After years of research, Dr. Lozanov found that it is not lack of intellectual capacity that prevents learning so much as the stress and tension of emotional blockage.[5] Stress and tension are especially evident at school and in the work place.

Picture a young student sitting at his school desk. Imagine what he might be wearing and what color his hair is. Notice the bored look on his face and his blank Orphan Annie eyes. Can you imagine what might be going on in his mind? Perhaps that morning, his alcoholic father yelled at him and put him down. On the way to school he is teased by a classmate for being different.

As he enters the classroom, his teacher points at him and, in a harsh voice, reprimands him for being late. His world does not feel safe. He is not hearing a word his teacher or classmates are saying. He is feeling bad about himself. The tears are welling up inside him, but he cannot let them out. He is confused. He can't think straight. His body feels cold and clammy. He notices that his fists are clenched. He would like to punch his father, his classmate and his teacher right in the nose. But he can't tell anyone how he is feeling. So he gets D's and F's in school. His face is fixed in a neutral expression that doesn't tell anybody anything about who he really is.

Now imagine a business executive, intelligent and attractive. Perhaps she is dressed in a suit and a brightly-colored scarf. It is Monday morning and she has had a trying weekend. She has told her husband she is leaving him. The children are very upset about it. The cat has run away and her house is a shambles. And she never did finish the project that was due today.

As she sits at her desk trying to finish the project, she feels an achiness all through her neck and shoulders. Her brain feels like scrambled eggs. Every time an idea comes up, it gets squashed by an image of an angry fist. As bright as she is, she cannot think of a single new idea. She can't even write an intelligible sentence. Worst of all, she begins to feel like a failure. But she can't let anyone know that. So she ends up with a set expression on her face and a voice that sounds like her vocal chords are tied in a knot.

Aside from the imminent crises happening in their lives, the young student and the successful businesswoman are also blocked by past trauma and old feelings and memories they have suppressed. They are not connected to their feeling side. In order for them to learn and retain information and to be creative and inventive, they will need to access their feelings and learn how to express them.

When I work with music and imagery, I often feel in awe of the music. It seems to lead the listener gently by the heart and guide her or him into unknown and unexplored recesses of the unconscious. These inner places are often areas a person might be too fearful to explore without the supportive cushion of the music. With a trained facilitator to guide the process, as in GIM, there is even more support.

Since music reflects the state of consciousness, it may bring to awareness, in the form of visual or feeling images, the fears, angers, hostilities and guilts the listener has been carrying around inside himself or herself.

It is these repressed feelings that may be at the root of her or his inability to transcend his physical, material reality and begin to deal with his spiritual development, as well as coping with the daily trauma of getting through the day.

In her timely book, *When Society Becomes an Addict,* Anne Wilson Schaef describes alienation from feelings and addiction as a vicious circle.

> *An addiction keeps us unaware of what is going on inside us. We do not have to deal with our anger, pain, depression, confusion, or even our joy and love, because we do not feel them, or we feel them only vaguely. We stop relying on our knowledge and our senses and start relying on our confused perceptions to tell us what we know and sense. In time, this lack of internal awareness deadens our internal processes, which in turn, allows us to remain addicted.* [5]

Certain music can reflect our inner turmoil, our secret fears, our feelings of loneliness. It also externalizes for us subtle emotions we may not even know exist.

During one Beethoven symphony, you may find you experience every emotion—even the most subtle shade and hue of every emotion—that you would normally feel in a 24-hour period! Music reveals our emotions like an inner mirror, and enables us to express the feelings we might otherwise suppress. By suggesting sorrow, joy or anger, music stirs our own emotions and gives us permission to feel and express them.

Working with GIM, music travelers may experience an opening up of tightness in the chest and general muscular relaxation, as the music begins to wash away the wall between them and their feelings. People who have not cried for months, even years, will allow the music to embrace them. It speaks to the non-verbal places deep inside them, giving them permission to grieve or sob or kick and scream. Music is a psychological bath. If you immerse yourself in it, it can cleanse you of stubborn stains and the residue of past trauma that you may have built up like layers of thick grime. The Psychological Bath exercises at the end of this chapter provide practical experience of this phenomenon.

In our efforts to suppress our feelings, a dark cloud of apathy often settles over us. It is a disease afflicting our entire society. In my GIM sessions I see adults who are half alive because they have deadened their feelings for years. They have not only forgotten how to cry; they no longer know how to have fun. I see children in schools who haven't the slightest idea when they're feeling angry or sad, frightened or joyful. They simply clam up or act out, and no one really knows what's wrong.

Child or adult, when we manufacture false selves we deny our inner potential. We sever our lifeline both to our true selves and to the true selves of others. When our emotional pipelines are clogged, even the slightest flow of information cannot get through, much less the spontaneous flow of creative ideas. Then we wonder why it is difficult for us to learn.

Working with music and imagery on a regular basis keeps these channels open. As we get to know our feeling nature, we begin to develop a sense of self that will carry us through the crises and vicissitudes of life. Instead of giving up, we learn how to own our emotions and put them under control of the conscious mind rather than letting them control us.

When you listen to a piece of music at home, you experience myriad emotions, but most of them are being prompted by the music below the level of consciousness. The more we attune ourselves to the feelings evoked by the music, the more we learn about the feelings we need to release. The more feelings we release, the healthier and more balanced we become.

Using Music in Stress Management

A misconception about the use of music for stress management is that only calm, soothing music should be used; that music which brings up sadness or anger is not relaxing because it is not uplifting.

In actual fact, releasing pent-up emotions and unhappy memories is ultimately more relaxing because the body, the emotions and the spirit all utter a great sigh of relief. The music that evokes these strong feelings and draws them out of the body and emotions, like poison is sucked out of a wound, is often stormy and stimulating rather than relaxing. Karl Haas, who has brought classical music to thousands of listeners through his enlightening program "Adventures in Good Music," says, "Not everything that is uplifting has to be calm and soothing. We can be uplifted by crying. If we react emotionally, we may be uplifted."

Listening to music with the intention of connecting with your emotions is called *conscious listening.* Linda Keiser, a primary GIM trainer, connects the features of pieces used on the GIM tapes to particular emotional states they might enhance.[7] For example, in the tape entitled, "Emotional Expression," the first piece, the Brahms *Piano Concerto No. 2 (first movement)* could bring feelings of agitation out into the open. The voices in the second two pieces offer support for these feelings, and the last piece, the Brahms *Symphony No. 4 (second movement)* allows the listener to be accepting of his feelings.

Hal Lingerman finds that people need to air their anger sometimes and need to calm it at other times. He offers musical suggestions for each. For discharging angry feelings, he suggests pieces like the Beethoven Egmont Overture, the Brahms *Piano Concerto No. 1* and the Tchaikovsky *Symphony No. 5.* He notes that music that has anger in it tends to permit the listener to vent her or his own anger. For calming anger, he suggests *Two Concertos for Two Pianos* by Bach, the *Harp Concerto* by Handel and *Golden Voyage* by Dexter. Since music may either calm or stimulate, the listener's feeling state and experience must also be considered.

When I was lecturing in Mexico, an American tourist told me this story:

My grandson, Joseph, aged four, was busy at his favorite pastime, drawing fantasy monsters. Suddenly, the front door slammed. His daddy, Mitchell, was home. Mitchell walked into the family room, put down his brief case and went to the elaborate high fidelity stereo system. A moment later, the strains of the Brandenburg Concertos *filled the room with quadrophonic sound. Joseph looked up from his drawing, grinned, and said, "Daddy's mad about something."*

There are many pieces of music you can use to help you deal with anger, as well as with fear or sadness. Try out different pieces of music, and notice how they make you feel. Soon, you will learn which pieces you can use to help you balance yourself.

Music Activity #20
The Psychological Bath

- Find a comfortable place to lie down. Take some deep breaths.
- Turn on *Air on a G String* by J.S. Bach, or *Prelude to the Afternoon of a Faun*.
- Imagine that you are immersed in a huge ocean of music. Let the tones and harmonies of the music wash over you. Notice how the music feels on your skin. Let yourself go with the pull of the music. Float on the musical notes.
- Imagine that you could dive down into the music's depths. Invite the music to enter into your body through your skin. Send it to the places that need to be cleansed and purified, and notice how it feels.

Music Activity #21
Balancing Your Moods

Here's a way to get in touch with your feelings and exercise your emotions. Begin experimenting with the five basic selections from Chapter One, taking note of which music seems to match your energy at the time.

- After a stressful day's work, find a comfortable place to lie down. You might want to use a floor pillow and lie down on the carpet or on a futon, mat or couch. This activity may be done in a comfortable sitting position if it is not possible to lie down.

○ Using the iso principle, select a piece of music that seems to fit your mood. If you are feeling edgy, irritable or hyper, start with a piece of music that is not too quiet, so that you are able to resonate with it and perhaps give some of your anxiety over to the music. Later, you can switch to a more tranquil piece of music.

○ Listen to anywhere from four minutes to 15 minutes or more of the piece.

○ As you listen, notice any change of mood or feeling you might be experiencing.

○ If you're feeling depressed, start with a quiet piece of music that has a slow tempo, such as the *Pachelbel Canon* or the second movement from one of the *Brandenburg Concertos* or *The Four Seasons.* Then move on to *Eine Kleine Nachtmusik.*

○ If you are feeling joyful and want to celebrate, play *The Four Seasons.*

○ If you are feeling fearful or timid about a job interview or social event, play *Eine Kleine Nachtmusik, third movement,* before you go. Notice if it gives you courage.

○ If you are feeling tense and anxious, or if you want to calm your anger, see what the *Pachelbel Canon* does for you.

○ If you are in a dreamy state of mind and would like to wander away for a short vacation that will not cost you any money, turn on *Prelude to the Afternoon of a Faun.*

○ If you are feeling meditative or reverent, play the second movement of any of the *Brandenburg Concertos.*

○ If you have any pent-up anger, *Eine Kleine Nachtmusik, First or Third movement* may help you release it and lighten up.

○ Keep a record in your journal of the various pieces of music and their effects. After you have worked with the five selections above, try out some of the pieces at the end of this chapter, if you have any of them in your record, tape or compact disc library. You might also try some of the new CD's based on moods or themes, such as Laserlight's "Meditation Series," Deutsche Grammophon's "Adagio" or "Sensual Classics." "Stress Busters" by RCA Victor can calm you, while "Power Classics," on the same label may strengthen and empower you. Before long, you will know which music works best for you when you are depressed or grieving, angry or anxious, or when you simply want to celebrate life.

Don't forget that although certain pieces of music have a tendency to relieve stress and calm listeners, and others tend to stimulate and energize them, you may respond differently from someone else.

Music Activity #22
Conducting to Music

To release stress or negative emotions, or to generate energy and motivation when you have a project to complete, enjoy a conducting experience. Imagine that you are a famous conductor. Even if you have never conducted before, turn on *Eine Kleine Nachtmusik* or a Beethoven *Symphony–No.* 7 works really well–and let your arms and hands move freely to the music. Become Neville Marinner or Zubin Mehta. Be unrestrained in your movements. Enjoy yourself! When you feel loosened up and energized, sit down at your desk and begin your project.

Music Activity #23
Free-Style Dancing to Music

When you want to lighten up or celebrate yourself, turn on the last movement of *Eine Kleine Nachtmusik,* or the *Nutcracker Suite* by Tchaikovsky if you have it. Let yourself dance, leap and pirouette around the room in any way that feels good. Allow yourself to revel in the sense of freedom and vitality it gives you. Feel your inner child emerging, and don't worry at all about how you might look to someone else. This activity is by you and for you. Let your exuberance flow!

Music Activity #24
Music for Business and Professional Life

Business people who listen to classical music at the office have told me that they can gain new, more positive perspectives on old problems and can accomplish more work in less time. Anita Malapit, an Assistant Manager at the Anchorage Hilton whom I met when I was traveling in Alaska, told me: "With classical music, it seems like I'm not even working."

1. Music for Motivation and Assertiveness

J.S. Bach	Harpsichord Concertos
Beethoven	Violin Concerto
	Piano Concerto No. 5
Brahms	Violin Concerto in D major
	Piano Concerto No. 2
Delibes	*Coppelia Suite*
Haydn	Concerto for Trumpet in E flat major
Mendelssohn	*Italian* Symphony
	Violin Concerto
Mozart	*Eine Kleine Nachtmusik*
	Symphony No. 41 in C
Rodrigo	Concierto de Aranjuez
Sibelius	Violin Concerto
Wagner	*Ride of the Valkyries*

2. Music for Calming Stress

Albinoni	Adagio
J.S. Bach	Lute Suites
	Violin Partita in D Minor
Corelli	Concerti Grossi
Handel	Concerti Grossi
Pachelbel	Canon in D
Telemann	Flute Sonatas

Vivaldi	Mandolin Concerto
	Flute Concertos
Wagner	*Siegfried Idyll*

3. Music for Energizing Your Work Day

J.S. Bach	Violin Concertos
	Orchestral Suites
	The Brandenburg Concertos
Beethoven	Symphony Nos. 1, 2, 8
Brahms	Symphony No. 2
	Piano Concertos Nos. 1 and 2
Boccherini	Guitar Concerto in E major
Castelnuovo-Tedesco	Guitar Concerto
Haydn	Symphony Nos. 92-104
Mendelssohn	Violin Concerto
	Italian Symphony
	Symphony Nos. 35, 39, 40, 41
Mozart	Symphony Nos. 35, 39, 40, 41
	Divertimenti
	Flute Concertos
Smetana	*The Moldau*
Tchaikovsky	Piano Concerto No. 1
Verdi	Overture to *La Forza del Destino*
Vivaldi	*The Four Seasons*
	Violin Concertos
Wagner	Prelude to *Der Meistersinger*

Music Activity #25
Music to Match Your Emotions

1. Music for Solitude and Introspection

J.S. Bach	*Jesu, Joy of Man's Desiring*
	Cello Suites
	Air on a G String

Barber	Adagio for Strings
Beethoven	Piano Sonatas
	Piano Concerto No.5 (second movement)
Chopin	*The Meditative Chopin* by Roy Eaton
Canteloube	*Songs of the Auvergne*
Debussy	*Claire de Lune*
Franck	Symphony in D minor
Marcello	Oboe Concerto
Rachmaninoff	Piano Concerto Nos. 2 and 3
Vaughan Williams	*Fantasia on a Theme of Thomas Tallis*
	Fantasia on Greensleeves

2. Music for Empowerment

J.S. Bach	Toccata and Fugue in D
Beethoven	Symphony No. 5
Brahms	Piano Concerto Nos. 1 and 2
Mahler	Symphony No. 8
R. Strauss	*Don Juan*
	A Hero's Life
Vaughan Williams	*The Lark Ascending*
Wagner	Overture to *Die Meistersinger*

3. Music for Exalted States

J.S. Bach	Magnificat in D
	B-Minor Mass
Beethoven	"Benedictus on the Kyrie" from *Missa Solemnis*
	Overture for *The Consecration of the House*
Brahms	German Requiem
Dvorak	Symphony No. 9 (second movement)
Gounod	St. Cecilia Mass, Offertoire, Sanctus
Mozart	*Vesperae Solemnes: Laudata Dominum*
Schubert	*Ave Maria*
Various	Gregorian Chants

| Verdi | Requiem |
| Zamfir | *Classical Zamfir* |

4. Music for Meditation

J.S. Bach	*Sheep May Safely Graze*
	Come Sweet Death
Beethoven	Symphony No. 9 (third movement)
	Piano Concerto No. 3 (second movement)
	Violin Concerto (second movement)
Brahms	Violin Concerto (second movement)
Dvorak	Cello Concerto (second movement)
	Symphony No. 9, "New World" (second movement)
Franck	*Panis Angelicus*
	Violin Sonata (first movement)
Hovhaness	*Mysterious Mountain*
Mahler	Symphony No. 4 (third movement)
	Symphony No. 7 (second movement)
Massenet	*Meditation from Thais*
Schubert	*Ave Maria*
Schumann	*Traumerei*
Vaughan Williams	*Fantasia on a Theme of Thomas Tallis*

5. Music for Celebration

Beethoven	Symphony No. 9 (fourth movement)
Clarke	*The Trumpet Voluntary*
Copland	*Billy the Kid*
Gabrieli	Canzoni for Brass Choirs
Handel	*Royal Fireworks Music*
	Messiah, "Hallelujah Chorus"
Haydn	Trumpet Concerto
Marais	Fanfare
Purcell	Tune and Air for Trumpet and Orchestra
Schumann	The *Spring* Symphony (last movement)

Verdi	Triumphal Scene from Act II of *Aida*
Vivaldi	Concerto in C major for Two Trumpets

6. Music for Intimacy

Berlioz	The Love Music from *Romeo and Juliet*
Chopin	Etude No. 3
	Piano Concerto Nos. 1 and 2 (second movement)
Lehar	"Villa" from *The Merry Widow*
Lizst	*Liebestraum*
Mahler	Symphony No. 5 (fourth movement)
Mozart	Piano Concerto No. 21 (second movement)
Rachmaninoff	Piano Concerto No. 2 (second movement)
	Rhapsody on a Theme of Paganini
Tchaikovsky	*Romeo and Juliet* Overture
	Symphony No. 5 (second movement)

Notes

1. Clynes, Manfred, *Sentics: The Touch of Emotions.* Anchor Press/ Doubleday (Garden City, NY), 1978, p. 77.

2. Clynes, Manfred, "On Music and Healing." *Second International Symposium on Music in Medicine,* Ludenscheid, West Germany, 1985, p. 18.

3. Ader, Robert. "Developmental Psychneuroimmunology." *Developmental Psychology* 16 (4): John Wiley & Sons (New York), 1983, pp. 251-267.

4. Bonny, Helen, *Facilitating GIM Sessions.* ICM Press (Port Townsend, WA), 1978, p. 32.

5. Lozanov, Georgi, *Suggestology and Outlines of Suggestopedy.* Gordon & Breach (New York), 1978, p. 258.

6. Schaef, Anne Wilson, *When Society Becomes an Addict.* Harper & Row (San Francisco), 1987, p. 18.

7. Keiser, Linda, *Conscious Listening.* ICM Press (Port Townsend, WA), 1986, p. 7.

Music and the Multiple Brain/Mind

God guard me from those thoughts
Men think in the mind alone
He that sings a lasting song
Thinks in the marrow-bone

—William Butler Yeats

Recently, the Japanese decided to revamp their entire educational system. Japan felt that its university graduates were becoming clones of each other. Industrious and bright as they were, they were neither unique, creative nor original. They were not, in the true sense, well educated.

True learning reaches many levels of our being. It touches our hearts, stirs our souls, digs deep into our psyches to dredge up rich sources of creative treasure or bring us face to face with the dark, elusive shadow images we have been disowning. True learning—learning on an inner level, not just the logical, reasoning mechanisms of our brains—involves all layers and both hemispheres of the brain, the conscious and unconscious mind, and the various aspects of our being that are activated through them, such as the body, emotions and spirit.

The Great Brain Robbery

Addressing only our intellectual aspects limits us by backing us into one small corner of our capacity. By trying to teach the brain how to function instead of teaching in accord with the natural functioning of the brain, we end up using only a fraction of our mental powers. As we begin to re-examine the way we learn, we awaken dormant faculties such as intuition and imagination, faculties which narrow "back to basics" attitudes have all but erased from our classrooms. We can learn to choose whether we want an open system or a closed system for our children.

In his book *Openmind, Wholemind,* Bob Samples defines an open-system educational experience as a flexible one in which students *explore relationships between things.* In an open system, fantasies, dreams and feelings are vital ingredients of the learning process. A closed system, on the other hand, is rigid and confined, focusing on "the right answer." Reliance on rational, conscious thought, a disorder Samples calls "Rational Neurosis," often keeps us from more adventurous and dynamic ways to nourish the brain and nurture a love for learning.

Understanding the natural openness of our brain/mind design encourages us to seek ways to liberate and stimulate the whole person, and move beyond imitation to innovation. Students are best nourished when they are enticed by a complex menu offering a spread of rich flavors, colors and textures, rather than being spoon-fed the same dull, one-course meal. The more choice and variety we offer them, the more they will choose to take in, and the more easily it will be digested.

Many parents and teachers know very little about how the brain functions, and children are taught even less. As a result, certain assumptions have been made about how we learn, and these assumptions have formed the foundation of our educational systems.

One such premise is that we learn only with our conscious attention. Although *more than 90 percent of learning takes place on levels below the conscious threshold,*[1] we have still not acknowledged the impact of the unconscious mind on learning. By ignoring this huge arena of rich imagery and hidden memories, we leave buried a treasure trove of creative and original ideas and resources that are naturally available to every unique individual. To unearth this treasure, the first thing to do is recognize it. Rather than being afraid to touch it, or pretending it isn't there, this inner storehouse must be acknowledged. Then we can learn how to bring it up to the surface through music and imagery.

The other assumption educators make is that we learn only with the linear, left hemisphere of our brain, which is best at handling details. It is assumed that if you learn one fact or skill intellectually, and add another and then another on top of that one, as though you were building with bricks, eventually you will end up with the whole building, i.e. understanding the whole concept. This is how most of us are taught or teach ourselves, and, in most cases, it does not work. Even if we learn the information, we are apt to forget it very quickly because we learned it in a fragmented, isolated way. After a number of these unsuccessful learning experiences, we conclude that we just have a poor memory, or the class is too difficult.

The good news is that it isn't our fault! Our learning failures have very little to do with our level of intelligence. They are more directly related to how we have been taught. The brain cannot effectively process information that is not meaningful. The input of the right hemisphere, which is best at seeing patterns with its global, holistic perspective, is essential in synthesizing the details and separate elements into a meaningful whole. When these independently-functioning halves of our brain work in co-operation and integration, we may suddenly find our memories vastly improved.

Music facilitates the integration of the left and right hemispheres of the brain in several ways. Neuroscientists have found that music activates the flow of neural impulses across the corpus callosum, the fibrous tissue that connects the two hemispheres, creating a harmonious interchange between them. Because the rhythms of your body synchronize themselves to the beat of the music you're listening to, you can do strenuous mental work and still feel relaxed.

In their studies on music and the brain, M. Critchley and R. A. Hensen report that music, because it is non–verbal, reaches the limbic system–a primitive pre-verbal part of our brain–directly affecting our emotional as well as physiological responses, such as heart rate, blood pressure and body temperature. They found that by activating the flow of stored memories across the corpus collosum, music enhances whole brain integration. These researchers now believe that music may be able to stimulate endorphins, natural opiates secreted by the portion of the brain known as the hypothalamus.[2]

Music also helps us let go of rigid thinking patterns. Because it reaches the non-verbal places in us and stimulates our intuitive, creative side, it releases the dominance of our more logical, critical left brain. When this happens, normally inhibited thoughts and feelings can surface. Lisa Summer, a Fellow and trainer of the Institute for Music and Imagery, uses music with children to stimulate right-brain thinking. She recommends that music imaging be used at various times throughout the school day to help children express deep feelings and thoughts. These "tuning-up" activities can be compared to the tuning of an orchestra:

> *Just as the musicians prepare their instruments for playing, each child prepares his mind and body, which is his instrument for learning. In the classroom, the children can now concentrate on the academics without interruption from thoughts about home, or tensions or unconscious problems.[3]*

In addition to exercising right-brain thinking, an even higher level of integration can be reached by incorporating Music Imaging activities into the curriculum, as illustrated in Chapter Nine. These become yet more powerful in the framework of a stress-free, accelerated learning program. In this system, many aspects of instruction are organized and orchestrated so that all of the brain/mind and the whole personality may participate in an experience that excites and motivates our natural thirst for learning.

Our Three-Layered, Two-Sided Brain

In addition to fluctuating between the two hemispheres of the brain, our attention also moves its point of concentration up and down through three different levels. The Triune Brain theory, developed by Paul McLean of the National Institutes for Health, is based on the way the brain evolved.

McLean believes that we actually have three uniquely structured brains. Each responds differently to incoming information. The *reptilian brain* is the oldest layer of the brain and contains rich symbolic experience. It is concerned with territory and the "fight or flight" syndrome and handles physical or sensory motor imagery. It responds to routine or ritual: the shape of a church or a king's crown. The music of Bach often evokes this kind of primal imagery. The music sessions of an accelerated learning class directly address this non-verbal part of the brain.

The next stop on the evolutionary spiral: as we began to relate to others, we developed our mammalian brain or *limbic system*. This layer of the brain handles internal images and emotions. In order to address this layer of the brain, incoming information must be emotionally charged. Music, because it is non-verbal, can flow through the auditory cortex directly to the midbrain network that is stimulated by emotional experiences. It uncovers the emotion-rousing properties of thought in order to evoke memories and weave them into current life experiences.

The *neocortex,* which takes up most of the skull, has grown so large that it dwarfs the other layers by far. It is the center for intellectual and abstract mental activity, and contains the left and right hemispheres. Until recently, scientists believed that this was the only functioning layer of the brain. For many years, educators have been addressing instruction only to this intellectual layer, which has been dominated by its verbal, logical left hemisphere.

However, the deeper layers of our brain are still functional, and essential for effective education. Only if these layers connect with each other will the material we're learning be meaningful, and therefore, remembered. According to Joseph Chilton Pearce, educator and authority on child development, "the sensory information coming in through our old brain is given its meaningful shape through the emotional energy of the mid-brain—it ties together the physical and the thinking brain."[4]

Cultivating a Naturally Good Memory

Margaret Mead had a spectacular memory. According to Jean Houston, who observed her when Mead was a guest in her home, Mead could remember just about everything she ever learned. She had been trained, as a child, to use as many sensory modalities as possible when she memorized something. She would see, hear, feel and even taste or smell everything she experienced. If she were learning a poem about the ocean, for example, she would close her eyes and see the ocean with her inner eye. She would hear the waves crashing on the shore. She would smell the ocean air. Simultaneously she would feel all of the emotions connected with this experience. Houston calls this sense of total participation and presence "attending your life."

Memory becomes much more vivid when imagery and emotion are involved, and thus more easily triggered whenever you need it. It is then reaching all layers and both hemispheres of the brain. Wilder Penfield discovered that, by stimulating the brain with an electrode, a certain memory may be triggered. With that memory all associated emotions will rush in, along with visual, auditory and/or olfactory sensations.[5]

If, for example, your first visit to Disneyland meant a great deal to you, you might vividly relive the experience. You might see all the people, including yourself, on your first roller coaster ride. You would feel the excitement, hear the laughter and screams. You might even smell hot dogs or taste the creamy richness of chocolate ice cream. The more emotion and sensory stimulation associated with the learning experience, the more deeply it will be encoded—and the easier it will be to access later.

Lozanov believes that memory is a natural, effortless function of the brain/mind. He structures learning to enable both children and adults to participate in a joyful, exhilarating and successful experience. As young children, we all took in our experience of the world in this vibrant, colorful way. As we grew older, most of us were not encouraged, by our teachers or our culture in general, to foster the sense of wonder that made every childhood experience intense and lucid.

Lozanov's method of accelerated, stress-free learning revealed an entirely new pattern of memory based on broader brain/mind involvement. He developed a foreign language program in which it is possible to learn over 1,000 words, used in context, in natural conversation, in a 72-hour time frame—and have fun doing it! By flooding the left hemisphere and conscious mind with large amounts of information, spontaneity, intuition and creative resources come to the fore. In most traditional courses, students memorize words but then forget them very quickly. Without sensory and emotional stimulation, the material is held in short-term memory only. In contrast, when students using Lozanov's method of role-play, games, songs and classical music were tested a year later, *even those that had not used or practiced the language at all were shown to have retained over 60% of what they had learned.*

Symphony of the Brain

According to Dr. Lynn Nadel of the University of Arizona at Tucson, there are two kinds of learning systems in the brain. The first kind, which involves the forming of habits and skills, is rigid, narrow and non-contextual. People with amnesia, for instance, who are deficient in learning relationships and are unable to draw upon memories, are still able to learn a skill through this first learning system.

The second learning system is much more complex, and involves multiple relationships and connections. This information is stored in the brain in such a way that it is part of a large relational network. It is possible to access it through many different paths, which are called *multiple retrieval routes.* If we provide the stimuli to engage this multiple network, we create the possibility of new routes to the information. Unlike the first system, if one path doesn't work, we can try another.

No longer do neuroscientists believe that individual nerve cells are highly specialized. We cannot compare the brain to a computer, since it does not work in linear sequence. Instead, the brain is much more global than we had previously thought. Every neuron is influenced by the whole system, and it appears that each portion of the brain contains the information of the whole. This concept is called holonomy, and is based on the discovery that the information of the whole is contained in each part.

Just as quantum theory views the world as a great jigsaw puzzle whose pieces exist and have meaning in relationship to each other, holonomy implies that oneness is built right into our structure. We can no longer deny our interconnectedness. From one subatomic particle dancing with another, to two human beings interacting with each other, everything in the universe carries the structure of the whole universe within it, as well as its own unique identity.

The word *holonomy* comes from the same root as the word *hologram*. A hologram is a visual representation of frequency patterns. It is produced by photographing an object using a laser. When the film is developed, it looks like a meaningless collection of dots, specks and swirls. However, when a laser light is again shined through it, the wave patterns captured on the film are released. This produces a three-dimensional frequency image, the hologram. If you look at it from different angles, you can see around the image or behind it; you can see much more than you could in a regular photograph. But the truly startling feature of a hologram is that when it is cut into pieces, even the tiniest piece contains the entire picture. This physical representation of the principle that *the whole is contained in the parts* has had profound implications in fields far beyond physics.

Based on the hologram, Karl Pribram of Stanford University created a holographic model of the human brain that has shed light on how memories are stored and how we perceive things. This theory explains why a person with brain damage resulting from an accident or surgery can recover the use of functions previously thought to be localized in the damaged area. George Leonard has this to say about Pribram's theory:

> *He points out that holographic encoding is particularly advantageous in the brain. As we've seen, it produces great resistance to damage, since an entire image can be reconstructed from the very small pieces of the hologram. It provides a most efficient means of memory storage. (A hundred million bits of information have been stored in a one-millimeter fragment of a physical hologram.) It creates a handy system of cross-referencing and association.*[6]

Brain systems are highly integrated. At one time, it was believed that specific areas of the brain responded to certain sensory modes of learning, such as visual, auditory or kinesthetic. Today scientists feel that there may he as many as fifteen separate areas in the brain where the visual mode is represented. Information from many sensory modalities may converge into a blending of the senses called synesthesia. These combined modalities may then mix with memories to create a rich source of stimulation for creativity and inspiration.

In Walt Disney's movie *Fantasia,* Disney piqued the senses with his revolutionary use of animated images set to classical music. Mickey Mouse, with pail and mop, set to *The Sorcerer's Apprentice,* and the troglodytes, lifting heavy rocks to *Night On Bald Mountain,* have become indelible memories for millions of movie goers. These are examples of synesthesia, and their ability to stick in our memories gives us an important clue to understanding how learning happens.

Music is a powerful agent for stimulating synesthesia. Patterns of music are translated in the brain into electrical impulses that may reproduce the same pattern in different senses. When we hear a certain pattern in the music, it may remind us of a visual image, a sensation or a feeling. This stimulates multi-sensory associations. Memories then blend in with this palette of senses and emotions, for it is the connection with our experience that gives music its meaning to us.

Dr. Bonny discovered that this kind of sensory crossover happens when the body is in a quiet state, thus intensifying the receptive energy of the other senses. This is why physical relaxation is an important ingredient of the GIM method. A client of mine brought the normally unconscious process of synesthesia up to consciousness as she listened to a GIM tape called Transitions:

> *When the shaft of sunlight came through the fog, it plucked my inner heart.*
> *I heard/felt the music. It was the feeling I was hearing. I used to look at*
> *flowers in a garden and I could hear the music inside me.*
>
> *It's as if I'm part of the music. Before, I would separate from the music*
> *and dance with it. Now there's no separation. It's like going on a sight-see-*
> *ing trip. Like being in the essence of sound: in the instrument and also*
> *inside the intent of the composer and performers.*
>
> *Every one of my cells is in touch with that music. I can taste it, feel*
> *every ounce of time in it. I can see the color it makes.*

Music can ignite the connections among the billions of neurons in the brain to set off colorful fireworks of thought, memory and insight. Because it is multi-dimensional itself, and makes itself available to us all at once, we relate to it in a more whole way than other kinds of incoming information. Unless we are trained musicians, used to focusing objectively on the various elements of the music, music pulls us into its flow, leaving us no time to analyze its separate components. Even if we consciously take it apart, its many facets are influencing us subconsciously.

The mental and spiritual exhilaration sparked by all these connections and associations promotes a fluidity of thought and experience not otherwise accessible. The highly resonant images evoked by these strong associations awaken latent abilities and facilitate our mental capacity. They stimulate our emotions and senses, opening windows of perception previously closed to us. As neural networks are strengthened through connection, they spark more and more ideas and insights. As deep memory is unearthed, music makes us think and feel simultaneously, so that feelings and information begin to merge in new combinations. The resulting inventiveness and creativity perpetuate themselves as they, in turn, form new combinations with existing material.

The music of J. S. Bach is extremely powerful at enhancing the frequency and integration of thought. At the same time that strong emotions are evoked by the beautiful harmonies and melodies, our internal rhythms are entraining with the precise Baroque structure to keep us focused and clear. We engage our older, feeling brain functions as well as our newer intellectual ones, and all levels of thought begin to explode.

Since the brain/mind has a wide range of processing tools available to it, several models of the mind have been developed to best meet the diverse needs of different children. In providing for the multiple brain network, we must consider whether an individual responds best through the visual, auditory or kinesthetic mode. If, for example, she or he learns best by looking at a picture, we can provide the appropriate stimulus for that child and help her or him strengthen the less-developed sensory modalities.

Not only do we access information through different sensory channels, but we also have different kinds of intelligence. Howard Gardner, in his book *Frames of Mind,* has identified some seven different types of intelligence. Linguistic and mathematical/logical intelligences, though they have been considered by far the most valuable intelligences, are not the only ones. In educating the whole person, other intelligences such as spatial, kinesthetic, intrapersonal and interpersonal, or musical intelligences are equally important.

Identifying a person's learning style, such as *reflective observation or active experimentation,* makes it easier for her to learn. According to Bob Samples, "…the broadening of experiences by a multi-modality involvement, the recognition of wider usefulness through multiple intelligences, and the application of the range of learning styles increase the likelihood of novelty in the solution of problems and the products of thought."[7]

The more we realize about how the brain works–and there is much we don't yet know–the more we realize that it responds globally and holistically to outside stimuli. It is, at the same time, a tool for analyzing and synthesizing information. The conscious, logical, linear activity goes on at the same time as the unconscious, spatial, intuitive processing. We simultaneously function at different levels of awareness: there really are no separate stages. Separateness was fashioned out of a mechanistic world-view that is no longer valid.

The genius of Dr. Lozanov was to create a practical learning method that allows us to blend our diverse energies by activating all the multiple aspects of our brain and personality at once, as in a symphony of different tone colors, rhythms and harmonies. In the accelerated learning class-room, logical/analytical instruction is presented in an emotional, imagi-native way, using dreams, puppets, stories, and similar non-linear teaching tools. The teacher organizes her non-verbal communication to reach the unconscious of his or her students. Music mobilizes latent memories and stimulates the emotions to create a powerful learning experience.

Turning the Inside Out

The unity of the brain/mind and the various models that help us to understand how it functions lead us to a vital question: what attitude can we, as parents and teachers, assume that will provide our children with the energy to keep their inventive wheels turning?

First, we can help them learn to express what is inside themselves. To do that, *we must value our own inner life and begin to explore its mysteries.* Young children, whose critical thinking skills are not yet developed and who function mostly in their unconscious, are able to relate to vibration and patterns. They are in step with their own internal rhythms. Their intuitive, imaginative faculties are highly active and they wear their feel-ings on their faces.

As they grow, they absorb the values of the culture. They pick up its obsession with objects and material things, and learn that those around them rely on the external world as a reference point. They begin to ques-tion their capacity to function on a more whole level. Their inner world then loses its value and they abandon it for the more "real" physical world.

Joseph Chilton Pearce believes that the rampant materialism of our culture emanates from efforts to reduce stress by amassing material objects. He paints a graphic picture of the effects of this enculturation on children:

> *We are perpetually locked into the external world. We ruthlessly deny the child access to his inner world, so through anxiety he locks into the physical world, anxious to defend it for fear it might collapse into chaos at any moment. He lives like an armored crustacean, on guard twenty-four hours a day, alert to guard his sensory world from dissolution.*[8]

Because of their attachment to the physical, outside world, many children never develop the faculties which lie beyond the realm of the physical. They never develop the capacity for imagination and intuition. Then, at the age when children are natural imagers, our educational system pushes them, too soon, into abstract thinking that is cut off from the images and graphic symbols it represents. Simultaneously, television does their imaging for them, so they rarely have to use their own imaging skills. *Encouraging our children to connect with vivid images of the objects or concepts to be learned,* rather than memorizing lists of objects, would make them more successful learners and more whole human beings.

Music and imagery can increase learning capacity through the practicing of imagery skills. Through music imaging, the energy used for abstract thought and higher verbal skills can be first directed inward, where it hooks up with rich sources of emotion. Without the psychic energy provided by the emotions, a thought is vacuous and easily forgotten. In order for children to develop the advanced abstract thinking skills of the neocortex, they first need to spend more time with their emotional, mammalian brain. They will greatly benefit by spending more time inside themselves in imaginative play. With music, we can help them focus inward.

Daydreaming: A Vehicle for Brilliance

Two of the most creative and brilliant men of all time spent a good deal of time daydreaming, in a state called *reverie or the half-dream state*. By submerging their conscious minds and allowing themselves to go into a deeper and more open state of consciousness, they were able to reach their creative resources. This is the way they solved problems and created new ideas and perspectives. Notice the way they thought, and see if you can imagine who these men might be:

1. The words of the language, as they are written or spoken, do not seem to play any role in my mechanism of thought. The physical entities which seem to serve as elements in thought are certain signs and more or less images which can be 'voluntarily' reproduced and combined. The above mentioned elements are, in any case, of visual and some of muscular type. Conventional words or other signs have to be sought for laboriously only in a secondary stage, when the mentioned associative play is sufficiently established and can be reproduced at will.

2. I cannot forbear to mention…a new device for study which, although it may seem trivial and almost ludicrous, is nevertheless extremely useful in stimulating the imaginative capacity of the mind. It goes like this: when you look at a wall spotted with stains…you may discover a resemblance to various landscapes, beautiful with mountains, rivers, rocks trees…or again you may see battles and people in action, or strange faces and outfits—an endless variety of objects which you could draw in all their completeness and detail. These images appear on such walls in a jumble, like the sound of bells in whose jangle you may find any name or word you choose to imagine.

The first genius, who thought in images, not words, was Albert Einstein. The second quotation comes from one of the most versatile, talented, whole-brained geniuses the world has ever known: Leonardo da Vinci. Instead of relying completely on rational thinking, they turned to inner experiences for problem–solving, and used them to enrich their lives.

These thinking patterns show a process very different from that which we, as parents and educators, impose upon our children. We expect them to think actively at all times, to express themselves verbally from the very beginning, and to take one-and-only exams that leave no delay time for the kind of associative play that Einstein and da Vinci thrived on. Inadvertently, we tend to cut our children off, by our expectations, from the natural imaging process that is part of their development. Associative thinking and imagery play are skills that are necessary for innovative, high-level thinking.

Music imaging activities are a fun way to encourage children to continue their natural penchant for playing with images and concepts as Einstein and da Vinci did. Many creative people, such as artists, poets and scientists, have a childlike quality that keeps them learning and growing. In order to foster this concept of "playing while learning," we, as adults, need to re-examine our old attitudes about learning that whisper over and over in our heads: "Learning is painful. Learning is difficult. To learn is to suffer." If we want children to learn with spontaneity and joy, then we need to believe that learning is effortless and fun.

Anthropologist Ashley Montague claims that he has been playing all his life. He reminds us that many creative people–artists, poets and scientists–are able to put together things that others can't possibly imagine, and come up with brilliant new insights as a result. Creative play enables them to risk unusual or unorthodox ways of thinking. Montague believes that we adults have certain traits of a child that we are designed to grow and develop into all our lives. Among the qualities of neoteny, or retaining child-like traits, are a sense of wonder, creativity, and inventiveness. Laughter and play are basic behavioral needs. They make us healthy, and renew our zest for change and discovery.

Joseph Chilton Pearce tells of a study that found that 3 percent of all children are both brilliant and happy. We can easily find examples of children who are brilliant but not happy, and all of us know children who are happy but not brilliant! The combination is rare. Children who have this combination often stare into space in the classroom as they are learning. Teachers often assume, when a child is staring into space, that the child is not paying attention. But that child may simply have entered into an incubation stage of learning: a receptive state of mind necessary for creative thinking skills to emerge.

As the teacher is speaking, such a child's brain is making all sorts of connections and associations. These connections enable the teacher's words to become meaningful enough to be stored in long term memory, and easily triggered when appropriate. While the student is staring into space, she or he may be calling up old memories and feelings associated with the new information. Her or his senses may be stimulated and she or he may even feel the body responding with changes of temperature or a faster or slower heartbeat. Even though she or he does not appear to be paying attention, the brain's neurons are making an infinite number of connections which are challenging and stimulating her or his thinking.

The more neural connections made, the more the brain is challenged—and the more efficiently it will function. This high level of organization of the nerve cells is what keeps us creative and productive. In order for us to learn to do what so few children do naturally, we need to give ourselves and our children permission to value imagination, intuition, emotion and playfulness—all innate faculties we generally dismiss as unimportant. Our challenge is to give up our attachment to achievement long enough to let ourselves connect with what is already inside us.

The Four Stages of Thinking

For years, we have known that reason is only half of the process of thinking. Now we can learn to convert that understanding into practical teaching and child-rearing strategies. Psychologist G. Wallis categorized four steps involved in the thinking process. The first step, *preparation,* is a conscious left-hemisphere process which involves learning facts, cognitive knowledge, verbal skills and memory.

The second step, *incubation,* is more holistic. It takes place in the unconscious and utilizes the right hemisphere of the brain. It involves relaxation, letting your mind wander, and preverbal association. This is the stage that has been virtually unrecognized by educators.

The third step, that of *illumination,* involves the left hemisphere becoming aware of the right, as in insight, intuition, and transition of images into words: the sort of process that Einstein referred to as the "laborious" step that follows intuitive thought. This is a preconscious process, in between conscious and unconscious. The fourth stage is *verification,* a conscious, left-brained stage that deals with cognitive reasoning, testing of theory, verbal analysis and critical thinking.

Two of these stages, incubation and illumination, require a quiet, receptive state of mind. Neither is addressed by traditional teaching methods. There is no space or time in the curriculum to foster receptivity in learning. Music, art, drawing and exploring inner imagery, although they help us learn how to perceive, order and understand our world, are relegated to the status of rainy-day busy-work. In many cases, they have been eliminated from the curriculum entirely.

This is a prime reason why many children are not learning successfully. They are missing half of the thinking skills they need: intuition, association and imagination. Fortunately, a more complete picture of the mental gifts we can foster to be successful learners is beginning to come into focus. As we recognize the global nature of the brain and its unlimited capacities, and honor the playful, bright, imaginative child within, the process of educating others will begin to come into alignment with the natural design of our brain/mind. Then the rough and plodding educational road will become a smooth path to personal fulfillment.

Music Activity #26
Integrating the Brain

The Little Gray House is a metaphorical story about the Triune Brain. The language used is designed to stimulate all the senses and reach the unconscious. You may enjoy this stories in several ways:

1. You may read the story silently or aloud.

2. You may read the story to Bach's Brandenburg Concerto No. 2.

3. A tape of the story read to music is available (See order form at the end of this book). Music, story and voice are orchestrated to evoke a powerful response from the unconscious. Listen in a relaxed position with your eyes closed, noticing the feelings and images that come up.

The Little Gray House

Once in a hidden valley there lived a strange and wonderful family of three generations: there was an ancient grandfather, a mother and her twins. It was hard to believe they belonged to the same family since they were all so different and did not look or act anything alike.

They all lived together in a little gray house. The extraordinary thing about the little grey house is that it was equipped with the most advanced electrical system known to mankind.

The ancient grandfather, Tilyan, was very, very old and shrunken, but he still had a say in the family. The mother, Mama Lala, was not a young woman, but she was very strong and she was bigger than old Tilyan. Her twins, Neah and Cort, were young and strong, but they were growing very fast.

They all worked together in a family business: information processing. Anything that came into their house had to be inspected and examined by all of them before it could be accepted by the memory bank. For instance, when the sun entered the window of the little gray house, old Tilyan prepared for it every morning with a special ritual. Every morning at six he raised his hands three times in a gesture of greeting. He treated the sun with great awe and respect since he had known its essence for thousands of years. He never spoke, but his presence was very powerful.

When Mama Lala looked at the sun, she saw it with all of her heart. Its yellow became brighter and grew more intense with each moment. When she touched it, everyone could feel its warmth on their faces and they felt warm inside too. Mama Lala never got burned by the sun, for she was a magician and she could make friends with even the iciest lakes or the sharpest mountains.

Neah was very much like her mother. She painted wonderful pictures of the sun. Sometimes she put a big smile on his face, and even made him wink.

When the sun reached Cort, he always did his job well. He loved to talk about the sun. While Neah was drawing pictures, he would stand in front of her and get everyone's attention with his eloquent speech. And so it was, he spent hours telling his mother and ancient grandfather why their friend, the sun, only came around in the daytime. He told them exactly how hot it was and that if you touched it, you could get burned. He also told them how big the sun was compared to the earth. Everyone marvelled at how smart Cort was. There was nothing he couldn't tell you about the sun. But he never felt its warmth, nor did he know its ancient essence.

After the sun had been greeted and treated by each family member, it was invited to stay with them all day, and to come back tomorrow and the next day. Each of them enjoyed the sun in his own way.

For many years they were equal partners in this venture, but finally, Neah and Cort got so gigantic that Cort decided it would be best for them all if he and Neah took over the whole house. Old Tilyan and Mama Lala were forced to live down in the base-ment, forgotten and ignored, and there they were hidden for many years. Neah was unhappy about this, but Cort said he could handle the business alone, and they would never miss the others.

But things were never the same after that. When the sun came around, it was not recognized in the little gray house. Its warmth was felt no longer, nor could its bright yellow color cheer the heart. Cort just kept right on talking about it, but the sad sun did not enjoy being in a place where it could not be recognized, seen, and felt, so it went away. The house was dark. But Cort still kept talking about the sun, because that was all he knew how to do. He talked only to himself, for now there was no one to connect with.

As for Old Tilyan and Mama Lala, as humiliated as they were, they refused to be buried at the bottom of the house as though they did not exist. Instead, Mama Lala decorated the basement with comfortable sofas and colorful paintings, and fresh flowers popped right out of the paintings and graced her delicate tables with the most wonderful fragrances. Old Tilyan built himself a room right underneath Mama Lala's. It was a single room with crude but solid furnishings crafted in the old ways. And there they both lived, patiently awaiting the day when the young giant, Cort, would realize how much he needed them.

Finally, one day, they heard the great creak of Cort's feet on the stairs as he descended. His head was bent low, and if he had been able to cry, he certainly would have. The darkness had made him feel so terribly alone, and he begged them to bring back the sun. He even invited them to come upstairs and live with him and Neah, but they were very comfortable in their own places. Besides, he was so big he often got in their way upstairs. Cort pleaded and pleaded, and finally promised that, from now on, he would always respect his mother and ancient grandfather for their vital input.

So each one stayed in his own room and did his own special job, but Cort built a wiring system between each of the levels so each one would know what the other was doing. Whenever Cort had a thought about the sun, he wired it down to Old Tilyan, who wired up its essence. Then Mama Lala sent a bright and shining image back up to the top floor, filling it with feeling. There, Neah would reflect its colors and excitement. Soon, the thought was complete, and there was a great celebration. When they began to work together in this spirit, the sun shone in their little gray house every day. Their faces began to reflect its warmth and its brightness, and they thrive on its energy to this very day.

♪ ♪ ♪

Learning with music and imagery is much more powerful than the presentation of abstract knowledge. A participant in one of my workshops commented, "I doubt I will ever forget the three layers of the brain and their functions. I have heard about the triune brain in other classes but I have never understood until now that the brain is really three brains."

What is there about *The Little Gray House* that makes the concept it teaches so memorable? It was created out of a metaphor, an image that represents the concept. Metaphors help students make connections and see patterns or relationships between two ordinarily different ideas. For example, a car that needs fuel to run is a metaphor for a person who needs food to function.

These techniques may be used to great effect by teachers. For example, a story intended to communicate the concept of synonyms, homonyms and antonyms tells of a family that has trouble communicating. Papa Homo Nym, Mama Anto Nym and Baby Syno Nym each seem to speak a different language.

A math teacher, whose ninth grade students found it difficult to understand simple first degree equations, wrote a story about the emtees of Algebraland who tied up the poor variables. Of course, the solvers went around rescuing them! A fifth grade teacher wrote a story about the functions of the major nutrients. The people of the land of Sapiens had built model living quarters. Mr. Pro (protein) provided a strong, solid foundation and structure, Mr. Hy (carbohydrate) was a fuel specialist,

Fatima (fat) provided maximum comfort and protection, Waterman (water) connected all the other resources, and Min and Vita (minerals and vitamins) were the power boosters.

This sort of approach to teaching concepts encourages the playful qualities and associative thinking that help children develop problem solving and creativity skills. In *The Little Gray House,* each character conjures up a powerful image in the minds of the listeners. The events that happen are charged with emotion so they will be easily remembered. The mammalian brain is being activated.

Many people experience anger or sadness when Old Tilyan and Mama Lala are relegated to the basement. Often, it brings up issues of rejection or loneliness for them. These strong emotions are then connected in their minds with the structure and function of the three layers of the brain. In the listeners' minds, Cort often grows to huge proportions, bursting through the roof as he grows. After the music creates even more connections and associations in the brain, the information presented becomes fixed in long term memory. Perhaps months later, with the mention of the reptilian brain, the image of an ancient and shrunken but solemn figure brings back a profound understanding of the silent but pervading influence of this oldest layer of the brain. The emotions that surround that image also come flooding back with that memory, so that this material learned becomes a part of the learner's experience, rather than an abstract, purely intellectual idea.

Music Activity #27
Music and Metaphor

Play at creating your own metaphorical story. Then set it to music. Here's how to go about it:

○ Decide what concept you would like to dramatize.

○ Mind map (or list) the characteristics of the concept. (A mind map is a visual, global representation of ideas or thoughts.)9

- Using the *Brandenburg Concertos*, brainstorm a metaphor for the concept.
- Personify your metaphor, e.g. the left hemisphere becomes Cort, the verbose, young, rapidly-growing intellectual.
- Give the characters names close enough to their scientific or technical names to act as a mnemonic device that will trigger the meaning behind them.
- Listen to the music you have chosen, perhaps *Eine Kleine Nachtmusik* or the *Brandenburg Concertos*, in a relaxed state, with the intention of stimulating ideas for your story. When the music has ended, rewind the tape and play it while you write your story.
- Read your story to the piece you have chosen as accompaniment.
- The more of the following ingredients your story has, the more memorable it will be:
  - drama
  - suspense
  - inspiration
  - emotional stimulation
  - humor, where appropriate

Music Activity #28
Music for Learning and Creativity

If you have never experienced it before, try studying to Baroque music. A therapist studying for her licensing exam recently mentioned to me that she was falling asleep over her studies. I suggested that she study to the Brandenburg Concertos. A week later, she called me, ecstatic, telling me that the music was keeping her alert and energized for hours.

For even greater effectiveness, summarize the material you're learning and organize it in short, melodic phrases so the right brain can relate to it.

If you have the time and feel like being really creative, write a simple metaphorical story that includes the major concepts you're studying and the relationships between them. Then read either the story or the summary to a piece of Baroque music. If you wish, record it on cassette tape and play it back right before you go to sleep or right after you wake up in the morning. These are the two optimal times to absorb information, as your conscious mind is still submerged, and your unconscious more active. Teach your children to do this. You may find that their grades and motivation improve.

The pieces below have been found effective for use generally in learning, study and creativity. The first list has been researched by Dr. Lozanov and found to enhance learning ability. It was created for the Lozanov foreign language classes.

Lozanov's Music for Learning:

J. S. Bach	Fantasy for Organ in G major
	Fantasy in C minor
	Prelude and Fugue in G major
	Fugue in E flat major for organ
Beethoven	Concerto for Piano No. 5 in E flat major
	Concerto for Violin in D major
Brahms	Violin Concerto in D major
Corelli	Concerti Grossi, Op. 6, Nos. 2, 4, 5, 8, 9, 10, 11, and 12
Couperin	*Le Parnesse et L'Astree*
	Clavichord Sonati
Handel	Concerto for Organ in B flat major
	Water Music
Haydn	Concerto No. 1 in C major for Violin
	Concerto No. 2 in G major for Violin
	Symphony in C major No. 101
	Symphony in G major No. 94
Mozart	Concerto #5 in A major for Violin
	Symphony in A major
	Symphony No. 40 in G minor

Mozart	Concerto No. 18 for Piano
	Concerto No. 23 for Piano
	Symphony in D major
Rameau	Pieces de Clavecin Nos. 1 and 5
Tchaikovsky	Piano Concerto No. 1 in B flat minor
	Violin Concerto in D major
Vivaldi	Five Concerti for Flute
	The Four Seasons

Other Music for Study and Concentration:

Boccherini	Guitar Quintets
Dvorak	The *American* Quartet
Handel	Harp Concerto
Haydn	Piano Concerto in D
Mendelssohn	Octet

Relax with the Classics Series:[10]

Relax with the Classics vol. 1, Largo

Relax with the Classics vol. 2, Adagio

Relax with the Classics vol. 3, Pastorale

Relax with the Classics vol. 4, Andante

The Optimalearning Classics:[11]

Baroque Music

Music for Driving, Dining or Doing

Music for the Imagination and Creativity

Notes

1. Pearce, Joseph Chilton, *Magical Child Matures.* E.P. Dutton, Inc. (New York), 1985, p. 135.

2. Bloom, Pamela, "Soul Music." *New Age Journal,* March/April 1987, p. 59.

3. Summer, Lisa, "Tuning Up in the Classroom with Music and Relaxation." *Journal of the Society for Accelerative Learning and Teaching,* 6 (1), 1981, p. 46.

4. Miller, Ronald S., "Reaching Our Real Potential: An Interview with Joseph Chilton Pearce." *Science of Mind,* June 1981, p. 19.

5. Houston, Jean, *The Possible Human.* J.P. Tarcher, Inc. (Los Angeles), 1982, p. 80, 85.

6. Leonard, George, *The Silent Pulse.* Bantam (New York), 1981, p. 71.

7. Samples, Bob, *Openmind/Wholemind.* Jalmar Press (Rolling Hills Estates, CA), 1987, p. 162.

8. Miller, Ronald S., "Reaching Our Real Potential: An Interview with Joseph Chilton Pearce." *Science of Mind,* June 1981, p. 19.

9. For more information on mind maps, see Buzan, Tony, *Use Both Sides of Your Brain.* E.P. Dutton (New York), 1983.

10. Tape available from: Lind Institute, P.O. Box 14487, San Francisco, CA 94114.

11. Tape available from: Barzak Educational Institute, 88 Belvedere, Suite D, San Rafael, CA 94901.

Nine

The Uncharted Unconscious

*The world of the imagination is repressed,
and the soul is left crying.*

-Marion Woodman

Many of our gifts lie, undisclosed, in the unconscious. The unconscious, that vast arena of hidden desires, repressed feelings, deep memory, insight and inspiration, has been largely ignored by educators. Because we cannot intellectualize it, measure it, or control it, we tend to dismiss it. Yet the unconscious contains the roots of our creativity.

Carl Jung maintained that healthy personal and spiritual growth are dependent on the integration of conscious and unconscious processes. Without this integration, we are estranged from a part of ourselves. On the other hand, if we embrace the unconscious, we can use it to enrich our lives.

Every time we communicate we are expressing all of ourselves, not just that part we are aware of. We are communicating, and therefore, teaching our children, on two levels at once: conscious and unconscious.

For their part, they are assimilating information on these two independent planes at the same time.

If we as teachers and parents are aware of those things that directly affect the unconscious, such as our body language, gestures, voice tone and facial expressions, we will positively influence the child's learning process. At the same time, we can help them by understanding that they already have resources of learned experience and certain patterns of thinking stored in their brain/mind. These resources are of unlimited scope, whereas the conscious mind is limited in the amount of information it can absorb and retain.

Romancing the Whole Mind

Our unconscious remembers things our conscious mind has long forgotten, or may never have been aware of. If you climbed up a flight of stairs, for example, you may not know how many steps you climbed but, under hypnosis, you would probably have access to that information. Smelling a certain kind of flower can bring back memories of a childhood garden, and you might feel nostalgic without knowing why. Later, a memory related to that smell might come back to you. Communicating on one level is like a juggler throwing one pin up in the air and catching it–when he or she is capable of juggling eight pins at once.

The unconscious memory is so powerful that Psychologist Stanislov Grof has developed an entire system of "holotropic" theory in which, he claims, memories of childhood, birth, and pre-birth are evoked through sound, music, and movement. Earlier in this century, pioneering American psychoanalyst Nandor Fodor came across several patients who had birth memories arise in therapy; when these memories were dealt with, the patients showed marked improvement. These memories had an undeniable effect on them: a man born on the Fourth of July developed a fear of firecrackers, and one who complained of being cold had been born during similar weather.[1]

Our unconscious mind is absorbing and storing this information, although we are unaware of it and it is not accessible to our conscious mind. It does not seem unreasonable to expect precise and detailed recall of information from a third grader when a newborn is capable of the same thing. The problem lies not with our brains, but with our methods of understanding and educating them.

The mechanisms of the brain/mind and its multiple retrieval system make learning on many levels necessary. If we are not communicating effectively at home or in the classroom, it is probably because we are not communicating on more than one level.

Art is a superb teacher precisely because it communicates on many levels at once. It can impart values, release emotions and balance you—all at the same time. Because its effect is indirect and subconscious, music has even greater impact. Because it takes on the reflection of your own consciousness, music is a link between the conscious and unconscious. It heals the split between these two often-divorced aspects of mind, and brings them into harmony and balance. The sense of unity listeners feel in the music results from integrating opposing levels of mind.

The archetypes or universal symbols that music brings forth from deeper realms help us tap into a potent source of energy. In symbolic form, fears can be brought up and released, as they are through fairy tales. This releases bound-up energies for constructive learning and growth. Archetypes can also activate inner strength or wisdom of which you might not have been aware. Music expands your awareness and widens your consciousness so that processes that are normally not trusted, such as spontaneity or intuition, are given free rein.

Since memory depends largely on the unconscious, music is able to stimulate it by penetrating non-verbal areas, where stored memories are normally unavailable for retrieval by the conscious mind. Forgotten ideas, buried in a subliminal state, beyond the threshold of recall, may be recovered by music. For example, there was once a musicologist who lost an entire manuscript he had written. Months later, as he listened to a certain melody, the contents of the manuscript came back to him and he was able to reconstruct it.[2]

Music allows time for associations to be made so memories can be triggered. Hypnotist Milton Erickson claims that when questioned, the human brain continues an exhaustive search throughout its entire memory system on the unconscious level, even after it has found an answer on the conscious level. There is also a delay time as material from the unconscious filters into consciousness. If we test students immediately after instruction, or give them "once-and-only" exams, we will not have an accurate measure of their learning since we are not allowing enough time for insights or "Aha!" experiences.

According to Lozanov, "It is stress and tension that prevent learning."[3] Tension comes from lack of confidence in the ability to understand, memorize and utilize incoming information. We can regain this confidence by learning to trust our intuition and imagination. An inner, receptive state of relaxed concentration induced by music slows down the brain waves, leaving the mind alert and able to focus. Critical thoughts and distractions subside. In this state of mind, the suggestion of the music is absorbed quickly, directly, automatically and intuitively, even though we may be unaware of its effect.

When a story or play is read to music, a complicated process takes place inside the mind. The open yet focused state created by music allows large amounts of information to be absorbed, precisely because the listener's attention is not narrowly fixed on the task at hand. With your focus on the music, the information is absorbed on the periphery of your attention. Its impact is all the more intense, just as the dramatic effect of a movie is intensified by the background music. (Who can deny the drama added to the Lone Ranger movies, radio programs and television shows by its famous theme, the *William Tell Overture*—and who today can hear that music without associating it with the Masked Man?)

When I was lecturing at a health spa in Mexico, actress Cecily Tyson approached me afterwards, very excited. She told me she had been memorizing her roles to classical music for two years. "It works!" she said, "and now I understand why!"

Numerous great artists have found ways to induce the state of relaxed concentration. Mozart needed to turn off his left brain chatter so he could clearly tune in to the music that was already there in his mind just waiting to be written down. At those times, in order to occupy his conscious mind, he had his wife read to him. Some of my best ideas have come to me while taking long walks. Other people get insights riding on trains or planes. Music creates this identical open, relaxed concentration, and at the same time, it uplifts and balances us.

When we keep the channels open between our inner and outer worlds, we remove obstacles that prevent an unimpeded flow from one state of mind to the other. Our natural propensity is to shift back and forth between the external and internal. Yet, we unlearn this natural gift.

Music restores it. Through music and music imaging, we can learn to slip in and out of focus easily, the way young children naturally do. Music evokes the state of flux that prompts original thinking. The ever-moving flow of music, its forward direction, and its constantly shifting patterns, make us more flexible even as we listen to it. Music, because it helps us to understand the world both consciously and unconsciously, can help us make the shift out of fragmentation into wholeness.

Intuition: A Direct Knowing

One of our most valuable, yet undeveloped, functions is intuition. Since intuition is an unconscious process, it can be activated by removing barriers such as excessive analysis and an overactive critical mind. According to Jung, intuition, along with thinking, feeling and sensing, is a normal function of the human psyche. Friedrich Nietzsche once compared reason and intuition to two mountain climbers at the edge of a wild stream. One leaps across on the boulders. The other builds a bridge and walks across with heavy, cautious steps.

I am not suggesting that analysis and intellectual activity have no place in the thinking process. A harmonious interplay between intuition and intellect can set in motion a rhythm that stimulates the creative juices of the brain/mind. Successful learning, as with Einstein and da Vinci, involves the input of intuition, along with the understanding and interpretation of it, culminating in its connection with existing knowledge. Music enhances intuition. Because music is immediate, and moves and changes all the time, it encourages us to grasp concepts instantly, without reason or analysis.

Images: Language of the Unconscious

Images are the language of the unconscious. In the receptive state of relaxed concentration, your mind is filled with images. Words begin to fade and images take center stage. They have a richness and presence that words do not have. In this heightened state of consciousness, your awareness is expanded and your mind can absorb a great many more ideas and experiences than usual. This is because images can represent large amounts of information simultaneously.

Images present themselves in a spatial way, not a linear, sequential way as with words. As a result, images convey in a split second what would take many words to describe. Words separate subject from object, whereas images fuse them. Through imagery, you can participate in and directly experience your inner world. Words are abstractions or reductions of reality; images are a direct connection with it.

Images represent our inner reality, so they are not bound by time and space. They contain a psychic energy that has transformative power to effect changes in attitude and behavior. Because of its potency, imagination was once revered as a sacred process. "Imagination or image-forming capacity," observes Robert Johnson, a Jungian psychologist, was considered a faculty that "receives meanings from the spiritual and aesthetic worlds and forms them into an inner image that can be held in memory and made the object of thought and reasoning."[4] These stored images form the basis of new, creative ideas based on what we have perceived and experienced in the past.

Images help us learn. They let us experience ourselves firsthand. They put us in touch with a primal way of knowing that awakens ancient responses in our brains. Within them lie multiple meanings; hidden aspects of ourselves and our aspirations; flexible playthings to be toyed with, given new color and shapes, taken apart and magically reconstructed and combined with other images.

Music is the magnet that reaches into the silent world where images live, and pulls them to the surface. As it releases them into our consciousness, we can use them to learn and discover what we need to know about ourselves and the world we live in. Classical music will normally generate a profusion of images. When you have a strong intention of inviting the music to bring you images, and you allow yourself to notice and examine them, you are then bringing them into conscious awareness. In this way, you can uncover your hidden yearnings and your unlimited potential for growth.

Creating Your Own Multi-Level Learning Experience with Music

Since I have been working with music and imagery, I have met a number of people who tell me they have always learned to music and attribute their good grades and lasting knowledge to this practice. Perhaps without realizing it, they have been engaging their many-storied minds. "Learning" is a broad term including aspects such as creative thinking, memorization, comprehension or the acquisition of a skill.

As I sit here brainstorming the various learning tasks that are strengthened and mobilized by the use of music, Vivaldi's flute concertos and their vibrant energy are setting my images in motion. Here are some concrete activities that are enhanced by music:

1. Organizing a project
2. Writing a paper or article

3. Studying for a test or helping your child study

4. Reading a novel or textbook

5. Preparing a lecture or workshop

6. Creative writing

7. Practicing Yoga, T'ai Chi or other physical meditation

8. Brainstorming a group project

9. Memorizing a speech or dramatic role

10. Creating a new computer program

Perhaps your favorite brainstorming music might help you think of some other ways you can use music for learning. *Baroque music,* in general, with its ongoing motility and rhythmic energy keeps your brain in motion and your thoughts clear. Many such pieces are listed at the end of the previous chapter.

As we have seen in previous chapters, music can be phenomenally useful for learning and study. Many people using Superlearning techniques use only slow or largo movements because their tempo of about 60 beats per minute slows down our brain waves and heart rate for deeper relaxation. However, Lozanov maintains that several slow movements in succession allow students to relax too deeply. Using the entire piece of Baroque music, with its three distinct movements of different tempos, will keep you shifting in and out of this deeper state so that you can maintain a sense of concentrated awareness.

Baroque music is also effective for organizing a project because it feels so organized and ordered itself. As you listen, you take on that organization. The music of J. S. Bach, such as his *Harpsichord Concertos* or his *Inventions,* is helpful for people working with computers or mathematical concepts. Once, at a workshop, I played a Bach concerto and asked participants to write the impression the music evoked. When I asked a young computer programmer if he'd like to share his impressions, he said, "Shhhh...I'm writing a new computer program!" The music had helped him crystallize an idea he had not quite known how to develop.

Creative writing to music often brings out deep realizations and profound thoughts. It can open up a flow of creative energies that surprise and please the listener. In the classroom, teachers find that children are not only more prolific with music, but that they write with far greater depth and creativity. Special Education teachers have noticed that children who are unable to write complete sentences learn to do so when writing to music.

A fifth-grader, who was getting D's in English, began to write in a completely different way when his new teacher started using Baroque music in class. He wrote a simple, spontaneous and heartfelt essay that won a national essay contest! Even if it had no effect on performance, music would still be valuable in the classroom, because children really enjoy writing when they do it to music. A number of children in a school district where I consult have asked their teachers if they could borrow a tape or CD to play while they do their homework at home. They often then ask their mothers to buy the same tape for home use.

The type of music used for creative writing depends on the effect you want to achieve. I often use the *Brandenburg Concerto No. 5 (second movement)* when I want to encourage workshop participants to reach deep into their inner selves and see what thoughts or feelings they can discover.

This music puts them in a very introspective state of mind. It gives them time to look at various aspects of themselves that they may have been avoiding or that they have just encountered. When we share the writing with the group, most people express their surprise at how different their writing style is. The thoughts and ideas seem to come from a very different place than they are used to, a place where forethought, analysis and logic play no part. The following is an example of a piece written by a woman who normally does not write poetically. She said it just flowed out of her:

> *High mountain lake ever so small…. Granite boulders hiding their secrets below the surface of the mirrored waters where sunlight dances, teasing the youthful grass. Evergreens silently growing, whispering to the higher self I*

*am trying to find as I lie on my back feeling the boulder's ancient story.
Where do I fit? Maybe I just do...*

When working at home or in the classroom with creative writing to music, first have participants listen to the music in a relaxed state, asking them to notice their images and feelings. After the music has ended, ask them to write their impressions. I usually play the same music again as they write.

Classical and Romantic music can be used for more lively creative writing when you want to stir up new ideas or spark the flow of creative energies. Again, it is important to listen first in a relaxed state and notice your images. Some of the musical selections I have found effective for this type of activity are Beethoven's *Symphony, No. 6 (second movement),* Mozart's *Eine Kleine Nachtmusik,* Beethoven's *Piano Concerto #5* or *"Emperor,"* and Dvorak's *New World Symphony (second movement).*

For young children, Grofé's *Grand Canyon Suite* and *The Moldau* by Smetana are very stimulating for creative writing. Try different pieces of music for introspective creativity and exuberant creativity. In your journal, note the effect of each of the five primary musical selections from Chapter One. You will be surprised, a year later, to realize how much your creativity and self-understanding have expanded.

Linda Keiser, GIM trainer and developer of the music and creativity list found at the end of this chapter, suggests 30 minutes of deep listening before embarking on a writing project that you may be hesitating to begin. This extended period of time lets you examine the images closely and make new connections. Often, new word patterns come bursting through. In determining the most effective music for creative writing, Keiser considered the particular instruments, rhythms and historical periods of the music. She found that the music she eventually chose facilitates writing, evokes new insights and perspectives, encourages experimentation, and enables writers to feel more positive about required writing projects. She found many therapeutic side benefits as well, such as improvement in self-image and increased energy levels.

When it comes to choosing and using music to stir the images within you, you will find, in many cases, that what will excite and spur you on may not elicit as many associations in another person's mind. This is the challenge of learning and growing through music. Keep trying different possibilities and keep a record of what works in most cases. When you strike the chord of creativity, your reward is a new sense of your many gifts and talents.

Music Activity #29
Practice Your Imaging Skills.

- Find a comfortable place to sit or lie down.
- Before turning on the music, establish your intention to notice the images it brings you and the associations that come up in your mind.
- Notice any feelings that may accompany the imagery.
- Imagine yourself in your favorite place outdoors.
- Turn on Ravel's *Introduction and Allegro* if you have it, or *Prelude to the Afternoon of a Faun*. Let the music carry you away.
- Record in your journal all the images, associations and emotions that came to you. Jot them down as fast as you can, without thinking about them.

Music Activity #30
Creative Writing to Music

- To get in touch with deeper, more introspective creative stirrings, listen to the Bach *Brandenburg Concerto No. 5 (second movement)*.
- Have a pen and a piece of unlined paper available.
- Listen in a relaxed position after some deep breathing and simple stretching.
- As you turn on the music, imagine yourself on a path. Notice what the path looks like and how it feels beneath your feet. Be aware of what you see around you. Then let the music show you where this path might lead.

○ After the music ends, rewind the tape and play it again.

○ As you listen, write about where your path led you.

One workshop I offered was held in Idaho's majestic Sun Valley. Two participants used the beauty of their surroundings to bring them to a point of stillness. In that stillness, they described the following states:

We are traveling across the vast white expanse of the northern ice cap. My dogs trot easily across the surprisingly friendly white carpet. A polar bear ambles across our path without turning to acknowledge our presence. We pass holes in the ice where seals swim playfully in water that freezes a thin film over the pool. As if in a dream, a number of flags, placed closely together, show evidence of past explorers wishing to mark their passing. As we continue casually across the expanse I am aware that the dogs are traveling completely without effort. Soon the dogs lose their identity as dogs and seem to be almost of the same species as I am.

I stood in a clearing witnessing the silent splendor of the first snowfall. The trees surrounding the meadow were covered with the soft crystalline snow, making them seem gentle and less austere. The crisp air tugs at my face, whispering of winter's arrival. Turning, a shower of snow crumbles from a bush as a rabbit leaves its safety, marring the pure carpet. Suddenly, I realize all stillness and life are one.

Music Activity #31
Enhancing Creative Imagination

Music to Stimulate Imagination:[5]

Beethoven	Symphony No. 6 or "Pastoral"
Berlioz	*Harold in Italy*
Bloch	*Schelomo*
Britten	*Four Sea Interludes from Peter Grimes*
Copland	*Lincoln Portrait*
	Quiet City
	Appalachian Spring

Delius	*Florida Suite*
Dvorak	*Slavonic Dances*
Haydn	*The Creation*
Hovanhess	*Mysterious Mountain*
Ravel	*Daphnis and Chloe,* Suite No. 2
	Mother Goose Suite, "The Fairy Garden"
Sibelius	*The Bard*
Smetana	*The Moldau*
	The High Castle

Music to Enhance Creativity:[6]

Creativity I Tape

Sibelius	Symphony No. 2 (first movement)
Vaughan-Williams	*In the Fen Country*
Delius	*Koanga:* "La Calinda"
Kalinnikov	Symphony No. 2 in A (second movement)
Yamada	*Aka Tombo*

Creativity II Tape

D'Indy	Symphony on a French Mountain Air (first movement)
Vaughan-Williams	Norfolk Rhapsody No. 1
Mendelssohn	*Scottish* Symphony No. 3 (second movement)
Faure	*Pavane*
Ravel	*Daphnis and Chloe,* Suite 2, excerpt

Note: These pieces are listed in the order in which they appear on the tapes, as they have been specifically sequenced for GIM use by Linda Keiser.

Notes

1. Chamberlain, David, "Babies Remember Their Births." *New Age Journal,* November/December 1988, p. 56-57.

2. Assagioli, Roberto, *Psychosynthesis.* Penguin Books (New York), 1976, p. 248.

3. Lozanov, Georgi, *Suggestology and Outlines of Suggestopedy.* Gordon & Breach (New York), 1978, p. 258.

4. Johnson, Robert, *Inner Work.* Harper & Row (New York), 1986, p. 23.

5. Lingerman, Hal A., *The Healing Energies of Music.* The Theosophical Publishing House (Wheaton, IL), 1983.

6. Keiser, Linda, *Conscious Listening.* ICM Press (Port Townsend, WA), 1986, p. 5-6.

Taking Learning Off the Page

In the education of the future, music for every person will be deemed as necessary as the reading and writing at present, for it will be clearly seen that it is a more powerful means for bringing life, health, and strength.

—Prentice Mulford

It is one o'clock in the afternoon. Two hundred kindergarten children are gathered together in the auditorium of an elementary school in San Diego. They are being introduced to their new curriculum unit on growing things.

Their wide eyes are glued to the front of the auditorium, where four kindergarten teachers, dressed as talking flowers with colorful paper petals crowning their heads, are sharing, in dramatic voices, what they need to grow: water, soil and sunlight. A fifth teacher, dressed in a bonnet, flower basket in hand, is playing the role of "Mary, Mary, Quite Contrary." She leads the children in a chant about the parts of a plant and its stages of growth.

The children, spellbound by their teachers' metamorphosis, are effortlessly absorbing the major concepts and vocabulary they will be learning for the next several weeks. Surrounding the teachers/actresses are numerous pots and vases filled with beautiful plants and flowers, whose colors and shapes delight the eyes, and whose fragrances fill the air. Famous still-life art prints of flowers, such as those of Van Gogh, grace the walls. A video of lush-colored flowers of many species is shown to a background of classical music. Then, as the children perform specifically designed movements that help them feel the learning in their bodies, they sing a song called," How Do We Know It's Spring?" which contains many new vocabulary words.

A visit to a second grade classroom finds a puppet named Sunshine, life-like in the teacher's hand, introducing a class on weather and the seasons. Sunshine is telling of his adventures in different parts of the country during each of the four seasons. He shares with the children his experiences with a tornado in Kansas, a blizzard in Chicago, crawling across the burning desert of Death Valley in California. His tale is suspenseful, exciting and funny. The children are taking in every word that Sunshine is saying, simply because he is saying it. They are in a state of relaxed concentration. They are not trying to learn. The process is happening effortlessly.

In a sixth grade classroom, the window shades are drawn. The only light comes from large flashlights which illuminate a collection of galactic posters. They are positioned around the room, including a few suspended from the ceiling. As the children enter, the first movement of *Also Sprach Zarathustra* sets the mood. The children are encouraged to wander around, taking in the feeling of the posters. As the music concludes, the class comes together to share the feelings and images the music and posters brought to mind.

Dramas, Songs and Games for Teacher and Parent

These are a few of the creative ways that teachers of stress-free, accelerated learning are using to introduce class material to their students. Through drama, puppetry, slides and visual arts, the major concepts and vocabulary of the learning unit are taught indirectly. Songs and games, too, are used. Designed for learning as well as enjoyment, they are chock-full of material that children assimilate easily.

Ten years ago I had never written a song in my life. Now, writing short, melodic grammar or vocabulary songs has become second nature. The teachers and parents I work with are amazed to find that they, too, can write songs. What's more, they love doing it! They enjoy discovering their own creative possibilities and, at the same time, seeing children learn quickly through songs.

The following song, written, as the kindergarten song was, on the plant cycle, is used in third-grade classrooms. It may be sung to any simple tune, or you can make up your own tune:

I'm a little seed
*In a **seed coat***
A seed coat
A seed coat.
*I **store** food*
in a seed coat
To make me big and strong.
*And bingo I'm a **seedling.***

*I live in the dark brown **soil***
The dark brown soil
The dark brown soil
Water** and **sunlight
Nourish me
*To help me **germinate.***
*And bingo, I'm a **plant.***

I reach up to feel the sun
*My **stem** grows straight and lean*
*My **roots** feel so deep and strong*
*My **leaves** are soft and green.*

*Now I'm ready to **blossom***
To blossom
To blossom.
I've grown so big
I can make more seeds
*And bingo I'm a **flower**.*

The most important words are emphasized and given special intonation while singing. Games can be played where children clap or hop on the underlined words. Movement may be incorporated as they pretend to be a seed, a stem, or the roots of a plant.

Here is a song, written by sixth grade teacher Beverly Garb of Seattle, and sung to the tune of "When Johnny Comes Marching Home." It offers an easy way to memorize all the planets and their order in relation to the sun. The students walk around in a large circle, rotating and spinning around a central student who plays the part of the sun:

The planets revolve around the sun,
Hooray, hooray
The planets revolve around the sun,
Hooray, hooray
The planets revolve around the sun
And spin on their axes every one
And they all go spinning,
Around and around they go.

Mercury, Venus, Earth and Mars,
Hooray, hooray
Mercury, Venus, Earth and Mars,
All whirling and twirling among the stars,
And they all go spinning,
Around and around they go.

Jupiter and Saturn are next in line,
Hooray, hooray
Jupiter and Saturn are next in line,
Uranus, Neptune and Pluto make nine,
And they all go spinning,
Around and around they go.[1]

Music Imaging in the Classroom

Music Imaging gives children permission to let their imaginative thoughts come out to play. A few years ago, I visited various schools to try out Music Imaging activities especially designed to help children internalize certain concepts they found difficult to understand. The second time I visited a second grade classroom, one of the children came running up to me after the session, very excited, and said, "When are you coming back? I can't wait to see what's in my eyes again!" This little girl had discovered an enchanted world right behind her eyes. It may have been the first time her imagination had been validated by an adult.

Most of the areas of challenge for children were related to language arts and English. One class had difficulty understanding the concept of synonyms, another the use of quotation marks, and still another, how and when to use punctuation marks. The Music Imaging activity which follows gives some idea of how it can be used in these areas.

Third Grade: Punctuation

Objective: To understand the use of periods, question marks and exclamation points.

Movement: Stand up and roll yourself up into a ball as if you are a period. How would you look as a comma? Now make believe you are a question mark. What would you look like as an exclamation point?

Imagery Focus: Imagine that you could travel to the land of Punctuasia, where all the periods, commas, question marks and exclamation points live. Pretend that they are alive and that they can do anything you want them to. Notice what each one looks like and what color they are. What do they do when they meet some words? Invite the music to come into Punctuasia with you and let the music show you what it's like in this magic land.

Music: Tchaikovsky: *Symphony No. 4, Scherzo*

Creative Link: Have students draw the story on large pieces of drawing paper with crayons or pastels.

Results: The children loved this activity. Punctuation marks suddenly came alive for them. Seeing them in a whimsical, more lively light made it fun rather than drudgery. Shapes of commas were everywhere. There were personified exclamation points. Some children drew trees with question marks hidden in them. Others drew the shapes of punctuation marks in the wheels of cars and trains, and in flowers and people. One saw clouds in the shape of question marks. Two little girls drew dancing question marks in different colors.

The music fit the whimsical mood with its light, staccato sound. As learning blocks began to break down, the children were willing to use punctuation marks more freely, and their improved skills showed up in the compositions they wrote.

The Magic of Story

Just as you might try to enlarge the scope of your creativity by writing songs, you might learn to reframe dull, emotionless material by transforming it into a story. Do this for yourself as well as for children. Stories have a magical way of heightening perception. They open your mind to new experiences and concepts. You become engrossed in the story, particularly if it is read in a voice tone that is both dramatic and soothing. You feel as you listen, and your imagination is liberated. Music immensely enhances this process, as the voice tone connects the emotional content of the music with the emotional content of the words.

The Music of Your Voice

In our culture, we greatly underestimate the effect our tone of voice has on other people. Varied voice intonation lends a sense of intrigue, suspense and emotional charge to our words. The right voice tone can soothe and calm us in distress. Voice tone speaks to our deeper, older brain and thus reaches deep memory. The voice is the greatest musical instrument and, as the mind's vehicle for expressing the quality of the soul, it becomes a powerful creative force.

A poignant example of the energizing influence of the voice is Dr. Martin Luther King, Jr. Here, George Leonard describes his unforgettable experience with Dr. King:

> *His faintly oriental eyes glistened with ancient knowledge and he spoke of human destiny with the vehemence and majesty of music. The sermon ended, the prayer, the benediction.*
>
> *Unrecorded, the precise words slipped away, but the experience is still with me. King's voice had touched my every muscle, every cell, and I was never again to be quite the same. For what had entered me was not just words, but a majestic rhythm; the indomitable, ever-surprising music of the universe itself.*[2]

Obviously, Martin Luther King, Jr. spoke from the depth of his being. If we can learn to be ourselves by connecting with our feelings and expressing them through our voices, dry subjects become filled with energy, and children will remember our words.

As you practice reading to music, you will find that your reading becomes more and more natural and effective. You will also find that it is a wonderful way to relax with the music and express yourself creatively at the same time. As you test out various pieces of music, you can release stress and become familiar with the music at the same time. Soon your intuition will tell you which selection might work for a particular story or dialogue. Here are some combinations of story and music that have been used successfully by teachers:

Roman History
  Greek & Roman
  Gods/Goddesses
	The Pines of Rome, "Pines of the
	Janiculum," Respighi

Solar System, outer space cosmic themes	*Also Sprach Zarathustra,* R. Strauss *The Planets,* Holst
Spanish conquest of America	Concierto de Aranjuez, Rodrigo
Math Concepts	Flute Concerto in A minor, Vivaldi (first movement)
Weather and the Seasons	*The Four Seasons,* Vivaldi
Historic Events	*New World Symphony,* Dvorak
Classification of Animals	*Carnival of the Animals,* Saint-Saens
Rivers, oceans, and other bodies of water	*The Moldau,* Smetana
American History	*Appalachian Spring,* Copland *Grand Canyon Suite,* Grofé
The Plant Cycle	*Peer Gynt Suite,* "Morning," Grieg
Christopher Columbus	*Swan Lake,* Tchaikovsky
Explorers, Adventurers	*Ein Heldenleben,* R. Strauss

Musical Bedtime Stories

You don't have to be a teacher to read stories to music. Many parents of young children are now using great music to read bedtime stories. One mother/teacher wrote to me:

Music has proved to add an especially wonderful and soothing touch to bedtime story reading. I also began to leave the music playing while the children drifted off to sleep. Although the children didn't seem to require music, I did notice that they could repeat the stories with more ease than when we had no music.

Because I often read stories to the children on cassette tape for later enjoyment (like nap time or when mom's busy making dinner), I began recording stories on cassette tape with a background of classical music. The results were fantastic! First of all, the music caused me to slow down my reading pace, and use pauses effectively. The pauses allowed me to take deep breaths, which the children imitated, and we all practiced relaxation breath-

ing without making an issue of it.

I now find myself using pauses very effectively both in reading and in speaking to others. My reading and speaking have taken on more pleasing qualities. Secondly, we have all become more aware of the effect music has on our emotions. I find myself now choosing music which is more appropriate to the story, and even the kids have made suggestions. Our best effort so far is the reading of Tatsinda *by Elizabeth Enright, to a background of Tchaikovsky.*

Music Activity #32
Music Imaging for Parents

You can do Music Imaging at home with your children when they are having problems understanding the material they are learning or if they are experiencing difficulties with their homework due to stress or tension. Music Imaging can help them internalize abstract concepts by creating a personal relationship between them and the concept. It can lead them to a deeper, more feeling understanding of what they are learning.

Here's a way to try Music Imaging at home:

o After consulting with your child about it, choose a particular concept, skill or attitude he or she would like to explore.

o Create an imagery focus, such as a story, or a scenario beginning with "Imagine that…"

o Choose a piece of music that can act as a catalyst for this exploration. You may want to listen to several alternatives and then choose the most promising one. To help you choose, review your scenario or story in your mind, with your eyes closed, and notice what the music brings to you.

o In order to allow the learning to be experienced in the body, create a movement activity that resonates with the imagery focus and provides physical relaxation and release of stress.

- Provide your child and yourself with large sheets of drawing paper, crayons or pastels, or blank writing paper and a pen. Other media, such as clay, crafts materials or finger paints can be used as well.
- Do the Music Imaging activity with your child and share the creative outcome.
- Notice the impact this activity has on your child's comprehension or attitude. You can assess this through his or her behavior, verbal response, ease in doing related homework, or grades at school.

Music Activity #33
Creating a Story

To create a metaphorical story, choose a concept you want to work with. Using music, brainstorm a metaphor for this idea. Next, write an interesting, suspenseful story, developing the metaphor. Then, choose your music and enjoy reading the story.

When reading a story or dialogue to music, keep these things in mind:

- Let your voice be another instrument in the music. When the music is soft and lyrical, let your voice follow suit. When the music swells, let your voice become fuller and more resonant.
- Use short, melodic patterns of language with frequent pauses. Let the music tell you when to pause.
- Read a little more slowly than usual and enunciate your words clearly.
- Follow the musical phrases as you read. You don't need to know all the nuances of the music; simply let yourself feel the flow of the music.
- Read as though you are performing a dramatic reading or a concert. Let your solemnity and presence suggest the importance of the words.

Music Activity #34
Reading Fairy Tales

- Try reading any of your child's story books to music.

○ The following list gives suggestions for music that may be used for such stories as *Rumpelstiltskin, Cinderella, The Little Engine that Could, Hansel and Gretel,* or *Little Red Riding Hood.* You can use the pieces suggested, or choose your own selection.

Music for Stories and Fairy Tales:

Dukas	*The Sorceror's Apprentice*
Haydn	*Toy* Symphony
Humperdinck	*Hansel and Gretel*
Kodaly	*Hary Janos Suite,* "Intermezzo"
Mendelssohn	Symphony No. 4, "Italian"
Menotti	*Sebastian Ballet Suite*
	Dance Music from *Amahl and the Night Visitors*
Mozart	Symphony No. 25 (first movement)
	Violin Concerto No. 5 in A major
	Eine Kleine Nachtmusik
Ponchielli	*Dance of the Hours*
Rimsky-Korsakov	*Scheherazade*
Rossini	*Fantastic Toy Shop*
Tchaikovsky	*Sleeping Beauty*
	Nutcracker Suite
	Swan Lake

Music Activity #35
Music for Reading Stories

Introspective or Philosophical Stories:

Albinoni	Adagio
J.S. Bach	Air on a G String
	Brandenburg Concertos
	Concerto for 2 Violins
Debussy	*Prelude to the Afternoon of a Faun*
Grieg	*Peer Gynt Suite,* "Morning"
Handel	*Water Music*
Pachelbel	Canon in D

Adventure Stories:

Beethoven	Piano Concerto No. 5, "Emperor"
	Symphony No. 6, (first movement)
	Violin Concerto
Chopin	Waltzes
Dvorak	Symphony No. 9, "New World"
Haydn	*Toy* Symphony
Holst	*The Planets*
Mendelssohn	*Italian* Symphony
	Scottish Symphony
Mozart	Piano Concerto No. 21
Rodrigo	Concierto de Aranjuez
Smetana	*The Moldau*
Tchaikovsky	*The Nutcracker Suite*

Water Themes:

Debussy	*La Mer*

Peace and Tranquility:

Chopin	Nocturnes

Music Activity #36
Selections for Elementary and Middle Schools

Albinoni	Adagio
J. S. Bach	The Brandenburg Concertos
	Air on a G String
Beethoven	Piano Concerto No. 5, "Emperor"
	Symphony No. 6, "Pastoral"
	Symphony No. 7
Brahms	Violin Concerto
	Piano Concerto No. 2
Copland	*Appalachian Spring*

Corelli	Concerti Grossi
Debussy	*Prelude to the Afternoon of a Faun*
	La Mer
	Sacred and Profane Dances
Grofé	*Grand Canyon Suite*
Handel	*Water Music*
Haydn	Symphony No. 82 in C major
	Symphony No. 101 in D major, "The Clock"
	Concerto No. 1 for Violin
Humperdinck	*Children's Prayer, Hansel and Gretel*
Mendelssohn	*Midsummer Night's Dream*
Morning Moods	Deutsche Grammophon cassette:
	Peer Gynt Suite, Four Seasons, etc.
Mozart	*Eine Kleine Nachtmusik*
	Violin Concerto No. 5 in A major
	Concerto for Flute and Harp
	Symphony No. 35
	Concerto for Piano No. 23 in A major
Pachelbel	Canon in D
Respighi	*Pines of Rome*
	The Birds
Rodrigo	Concierto de Aranjuez
Saint-Saens	*Carnival of the Animals*
Tchaikovsky	Violin Concerto in D major
	Waltz from *Sleeping Beauty, Swan Lake*
	Nutcracker Suite
Telemann	Flute Concertos
	Concerto for Three Violins & Orchestra
Vaughan Williams	*Greensleeves*
	The Lark Ascending
Vivaldi	*The Four Seasons*
	Flute Concertos

Music Activity #37
Selections for High Schools and Colleges

Albinoni	Adagio
J.S. Bach	The Brandenburg Concertos
	Orchestral Suite No. 3
	Flute Sonatas
Beethoven	Violin Concerto
	Piano Concerto No. 5, "Emperor"
	Symphony No. 6, "Pastoral"
Brahms	Piano Concerto No. 2
	Violin Concerto
Dvorak	Symphony No. 9, "New World"
Handel	*Water Music*
	Royal Fireworks Music
Haydn	Trumpet Concerto in E-flat major
	Symphony in G major
Holst	*The Planets*
Mendelssohn	*Italian* Symphony
Mozart	Symphony No. 40 in G minor
	Symphony No. 41 in C, "Jupiter"
	Violin Concert No. 5 in A major
Pachelbel	Canon in D
Rodrigo	Concierto de Aranjuez
Smetana	*The Moldau*
R. Strauss	*Also Sprach Zarathustra*
	The Hero's Life— *"Ein HeldenLeben"*
Vivaldi	*The Four Seasons*
	Flute Concertos
	Violin Concertos
Wagner	*Ride of the Valkyries*

Notes

1. For other effective dramas, songs, and games to be used by teachers and parents, see Merritt, *Successful, Non-Stressful Learning* (order form in back of book).

2. Leonard, George, *The Silent Pulse.* Bantam (New York), 1981, p. 160–161.

Eleven

Unmasking Your Secret Self

Imagine the universe as an enormous puzzle. Each of us is a unique and vital piece of that puzzle.

—Anne Wilson Schaef

Loss of self is one of the most serious crises of our times. For years, women have been losing their identities in their children and home-making chores. Children lose their identities in the need to be accepted by their peers and parents. Even highly successful businessmen suffer from their success, depressed because they feel they have betrayed themselves by trading away love and integrity.

We are all too often willing to destroy ourselves emotionally and physically for material gain and pleasure. When we betray our deepest values, we throw our lives completely out of balance. Only if we put as much energy into finding and maintaining our equilibrium as we do in working for the accoutrements of success can our sense of self have a chance to emerge.

Identity crises are common when we feel so inadequate that we are afraid to show our true selves to others. But what price must we pay for the privilege of being our unique selves? Even when someone has the courage to accept being laughed at or put down by revealing her true self to others, there may be a considerable cost in more practical ways. The student who gets F's in school because she dares to think for herself or challenge the teacher's statements is the same person who may lose her job as an adult because she offers original and unorthodox input. She is "odd-ball out." This strange system of ours often punishes people for being different and original; it also rewards them for wearing the same uniform everyone else does, whether or not that uniform fits.

Discovering Our True Identities

Imprisoned in our ill-fitting personas, we often respond with self-hate, worthlessness, fear and resignation to whatever life dishes out, as though we had nothing to say about our destinies. Every year, it becomes more and more frightening to shed the uniform and strip down to our naked essence. What is most terrifying is the prospect that there may be nothing there.

I once had a client who hid behind his striking good looks. He used them to get all the rewards an attractive person can get in our world. But it never helped him feel any better about himself because of the fear that, beneath the surface, there was nothing substantial—no character, no integrity, no solid core. It had kept him back from learning to know himself. Through a series of personal sessions in Guided Imagery and Music, he discovered a part of himself that was "flesh and blood" and was actively pursuing its own purpose according to its very own belief system. It was not at all dependent on the outer world for validation or approval. He began to feel better about himself and was willing to risk looking at what else he might find beneath his good looks.

When teaching adults Spanish using classical music, games, songs, and drama, I had a student who was a swimming pool salesman. George was bluff, jovial and extremely macho. One of the more powerful strategies of Lozanov's system is that the students all assume new names and identities and keep them throughout the course. It allows them to free themselves from the personas they are locked into and to explore other possibilities. Businessmen often choose to be acrobats or scientists; stressed-out professionals often choose to be nomads, free to wander wherever they wish and sleep out under the stars.

George, the swimming pool salesman, chose to be a musician. Even with a supportive teacher and environment, the first day of class can be overwhelming because the student is being totally immersed in a language he doesn't know. George felt his identity, the only identity he knew, being stripped away, and it was an upsetting experience for him at first. As George, he was the archetypal salesman; as Rafael, the musician, his true self gradually emerged.

Beneath the hard, aggressive surface, there shook a timid little boy scared to death of making a mistake. His hands trembled, his voice quivered, his jaw locked. He did not know how to act without his facade. It took a good deal of classical music (played while the Spanish words were being received in the form of a play), loving support, and his own subconscious acceptance of my belief in his capacity to be himself, to turn him around. As soon as he began to get comfortable with the self he had stifled, he learned a lot of Spanish. More important, he found out that he wasn't who he thought he was. By being someone else for a little while, he discovered his true identity.

Children Need Help, Too

Children should not have to wait until they grow up to experience the various aspects of their personalities and begin to integrate them. They need not go through their childhoods feeling inadequate because they see only the parts of themselves that have disappointed others.

Being exposed to Music Imaging sessions early in their lives allows them to experience themselves in a positive way from the very beginning.

Unlike the more conscious, directed self-esteem exercises being practiced in some homes and schools, Music Imaging does not impose someone else's affirmations on them. It allows rich material to surface from the unconscious, unique for every individual, that will show them their hidden strengths and possibilities. Then, when they are coping with difficult issues in their lives, they can call upon a particular image to support them and give them strength and courage. They will know that they carry that positive energy and support within themselves—that it need not come from outside them.

Music Imaging directed toward building self-esteem may be done in the home as a pleasant, relaxing and educational way to spend time with your child. In the classroom, Music Imaging can allow children to physically feel a particular piece of information on a deeper level, and at the same time, experience themselves in a new way.

Some time ago, I visited a third-grade classroom in connection with my consulting work. It was in the Willowbrook section of Los Angeles, and I suggested during the activity that the children might imagine they were meeting Martin Luther King, Jr. Lakeesha, a silent, rather shy child who had not participated much up until then, imaged that she had shaken his hand, and that he had given her a locket.

Then, she told the class, she had met Harriet Tubman, the black ex-slave who had led many slaves, at great danger to herself, to freedom in the north on the underground railroad. Tubman had given her a pair of magical shoes. And finally, Janet Jackson had sung a song especially for her, and given her an autographed picture!

Lakeesha now really felt good about herself. She felt that there must have been something about her that deserved the locket and the magical shoes. In fairy tales and myths, these are objects that may be used for overcoming tests and trials. How supportive it could be for this little girl to visualize herself in her magical shoes the next time she found herself in a difficult situation! It would be especially helpful because these images came spontaneously out of her very own unconscious. Lakeesha was very surprised when Harriet Tubman showed up. She had not been mentioned at all in the pre-music focus. This powerful black woman probably reflected back to this child some of her own vitality and potency, of which she may not have been aware.

A child's positive self-image is often reflected in his drawings through colorful, beautiful images, but beautiful positive images do not always come up for children.

Once in a while, there are drawings or stories that reveal a very negative self-image. Recognizing how bad these children feel about themselves is a signal that they may need extra help or attention from either the teacher or a school counsellor. If a child is constantly seeing her- or himself in violent situations where he is being harmed or is harming others, it might be wise to talk to her or him privately to gain a better understanding of his home and family life.

Changing Your Own Self-Image

Adults, too, can use music and their imaginations to alter their sense of self-worth. It is often humbling to watch them create magnificent scenarios in their unconscious and then bring them to consciousness as they listen to the music.

Nan came to me for a series of GIM sessions. Thirty-five, unmarried, working as an accountant, she dressed in muted, unflattering clothes and spoke so quietly that her voice was sometimes inaudible. The little she said about herself was negative; she was a woman with a poor self-image.

Listening to one of the GIM tapes I played, she was suddenly reminded of her grandmother's vegetable garden which she had tended as a child. She remembered it as being overgrown, the tomato plants looking dry, the garden needing a lot of work. Under her care it never became the picture-book garden she had meant it to be. She remembered feeling that she was not working hard enough to make it beautiful; she had often felt like giving up.

But now, as she let herself stand inside this imperfect garden, examining her feelings while the music brought her into a deeper state of consciousness, she began to realize how much pleasure the garden had actually given her. No, it had not been a vision of beauty, no, it had never been totally free of weeds. But she had watered it and tended it to the best of her childish ability, and it had given her pleasure. And it had produced a lot of vegetables.

"It didn't matter that I couldn't make it perfect," she told me. "It was mine, it was fun, and it made me happy." She now saw the vegetable garden as her own sense of self: imperfect, needing work, but productive. She learned to stop judging everything she did. She gradually became more self-confident, looking more relaxed and speaking with more conviction.

When she lost a contact lens just before one of our sessions, she came to my office wearing very heavy bifocals. She wore them again, several days later, and I asked her if she hadn't received her new contact lens yet. She laughed and shrugged and said, "Yes, I have, but these are so much more comfortable. And you know what? It feels good not to care what someone else thinks of my looks!"

Positive experiences through imagery can also serve as a rehearsal for real life experiences. This often involves connecting with a hidden aspect of the personality that has been disowned. Janice was 43, a pretty suburban matron married to a surgeon, overly concerned with what other people thought of her and heavily burdened with her life experiences. As I played the GIM tape, she related to me what she was imaging.

I'm in a high school gym. People are sitting in the bleachers listening to music. They're wearing graduation robes. It's kind of depressing. Others are walking around in circles; they're not going anywhere. I'll march with them. I'm not wearing a blue robe, though. I'm wearing a red dress. I'm flitting in and out like a bird. I'm not walking on the path like everyone else. I want to annoy them—show them I'm not doing what they're doing. I want to be obnoxious. I tweak someone's nose. They're expressionless; not fazed by anything I do.

I get on top of their precious academic hats. They don't even notice. I'll try shoving one of them. They're immovable, even though they're moving on their own little path.

I pull one of them out. I'm helping him take his robe off. He's a little kid. Now we're on a stage doing the can-can. Showing off. I'm glad the kid escaped. He's shorter than me with brown hair and round, blank eyes. He's wearing a little blue shirt, short black pants and big Mickey Mouse shoes. His skinny little legs are dancing. He's happy. His eyes are getting normal now. His big, brown eyes are looking at me; they have flecks of gold in them. I'm enveloped in them. He wants to rest now: I've tired him out.

The others are still marching in a circle. They'll probably do that forever. We leave the gym. That great big door slams, and we leave all that behind us.

This woman, who had seen herself as a conformist and people-pleaser, found herself experimenting with an aspect of her inner child that she had lost touch with: a fun-loving, provocative adventuress who dared to be on a different path and even to taunt the serious academicians with her teasing. Her antics with the little "kid" she pulled out of line and ran away with, and the feeling of being enveloped in his gold-flecked eyes, appear to be a further integration of her inner, spontaneous child.

Shortly afterward, her life began to reflect this integration. She became able to make decisions which she knew would not meet with the approval of her family and acquaintances. She grew stronger in her own convictions and used her natural playfulness and the connection with her inner child to help her stand up to societal pressures.

In Music Imaging and GIM sessions, poor self-esteem is often reflected in the kind of environment in which the traveler finds herself. She may be on a path that is slimy, slippery, rough, full of sticky tar, muddy or weed-infested. She might find herself in dark, troubled waters, or in a blue-green boat on a blue-green sea where she cannot be seen.

As the GIM work continues, these kinds of images become gardens in bloom or well-traveled paths that feel safe and easy to walk on. A traveler who started out suspended in a thick oil that felt protective but heavy, found herself, fourteen sessions later, in a sacred room of crystals, filled with reflected light. It was "a place of warmth, love, gratitude; a place of thankfulness and benevolence; a place of worth."

Support, loving care and encouragement are boosters of self-esteem. For various reasons, many of us do not receive the kind of support we need in the outer world. Nevertheless, we may find it within. Many women are able to find great strength when they begin to integrate their animus, or masculine energy. This encounter with a strong, assertive, supportive aspect of themselves often involves a male dancer:

> *I see myself as a ballet dancer; I know I'm the best dancer. I am standing with my mate watching other performers. They're part of the ballet company. They're good, but we're the best. We're not proud or anything; we're the best. We're supportive of the other dancers. We make suggestions as to how they can improve. It feels really nurturing. My dance partner is really supporting me—He's willing for me to be the star. He admires what I'm doing. I want to thank him for being here.*

Men, on the other hand, may find a great source of spiritual inspiration in an encounter with their feminine aspect, or anima. The energy released can put them in touch with their own limitlessness:

> *A singer is floating above the audience in a diaphanous gown. She has long, blond hair. She's wearing emerald earrings and a diamond necklace. The top of the dome opens up, like a flower. Everyone is floating out of it.*
>
> *The woman encourages me to follow her. She's rising up toward a bright light. The woman represents a spiritual call—a pied piper, and all the other people are empty shells—no substance. They aren't able to follow her. But I am alive. Flesh and blood.*
>
> *She's holding my hand and we're flying. There's a garden with statues, pools and fountains. We reach a big pinkish purple membrane; the boundary to that dimension. We fly right through it. She's showing me different possibilities. I can create anything I want to. She encourages me to have faith; confidence in my own abilities. Like going through that membrane. It appears solid, but you just go right through. I ask her if this relates to career and work and to my whole life.*

My self-limitation and fears are holding me back. I need courage to go through. It's as if my wings are folded, as if I'm in a cocoon. I'm slowly opening up my wings, which I have wrapped around myself. It's uncomfortable. Everything's folded up and I'm just standing on one little spot...

I see that my wings work. I'm diving off my perch and soaring. I can see a distant solar system. I'm heading toward it. I go through a bright light and come out the other end. It's like being a meteor!

Once this kind of energy is released, you feel empowered to meet life's challenges head on and become whatever you were meant to become. The energy in archetypes, or universal symbols, such as the beautiful woman with long, flowing hair and white gown, is especially powerful because it emanates from the collective unconscious and is felt at the very deepest level of our being where we are all connected.

The above experiences occurred in one-to-one GIM sessions, but even in a short, solitary Music Imaging session you may see yourself engaged in activities you would not ordinarily attempt: dancing gracefully in a meadow, belting out a song, playing an instrument you've never played in your life. Once you have experienced these things through imaging, you are more apt to explore new possibilities for yourself.

Music Activity #38
Letting the Inner You Shine Through

Get comfortable, with paper and colored markers and your journal.

"The Will in the Wall" is the last of the metaphorical stories included in this book. The language used is designed to stimulate all the senses and reach the unconscious. You may enjoy these stories in several ways:

1. You may read the story silently or aloud.

2. You may read the story to Bach's *Air on a G String* or Pachelbel's *Canon in D.*

3. A tape of the story read to music can be ordered from the last page of this book. Music, story and voice are orchestrated to evoke a powerful response from the unconscious. Listen in a relaxed position with your eyes closed, noticing the feelings and images that come up.

The Will in the Wall

Not long ago there lived a kind and loving woman named Nona. She passed her days in service to others, though they often did not notice her, for she always wore a brownish gray garment of heavy wool that covered her from head to toe. No matter where she was, she blended into the background as if she were part of it, and her eyes were always fixed on the ground beneath her.

One day, as she was leaning against the grayish brown wall of her home, feeling exhausted from the day's errands and tasks, the wall behind her began to quake. She heard a strange, hollow voice echoing from its inner chambers and resounding through her ears. It was the Will in the Wall. "Nona," it said, "You are no one, and you have never been free. You might as well come into my world, and become a part of me." At that, he began to absorb her into his flat and colorless world, as water is sucked in by a sponge. And there Nona was kept a prisoner of the Will in the Wall. And the saddest thing of all was that no one noticed she was gone.

The world in the wall was pleasant enough. Nona saw no one, for this was a world of mysterious sounds and voices. Aside from the booming voice of the Will in the Wall, which she heard every day, there were other more gentle sounds. Once she heard a tiny tapping sound and wondered what it was. Nona felt rather comfortable serving the Will when he boomed out his needs. But Nona's head was bent low under her brownish gray hood, and her eyes could see only the earth beneath her feet. Secretly, she wished she could look upwards so she could fill the blue of her eyes with the infinite blue of the sky.

One night, as she lay fast asleep, there was a tap tap tapping in the wall, and suddenly, the ten tiny women of the woodwork appeared. Each one was a mirror image of Nona, except that they all had heart-shaped ears and iridescent eyes of many colors that glowed red when they were angry. Their sharp, pointy noses began to twitch as their high voices screeched angrily. They jumped up and down on Nona's stomach but they were so light she did not stir.

In their anger, they began to tug at her brownish gray garment. They ripped and they ripped until all the pieces of the garment lay in shreds on the floor. Then they got very quiet. The twenty iridescent eyes were fixed on Nona with a magnet power, for there she lay, in a gown of sparkling gold that lit up the whole room. Her skin had a pearly glow and her hair shone like polished ebony. "Nona, Nona, wake up," they said. But Nona didn't stir. They realized that, if she were to wake up just then, she might be blinded by her own brilliance. So, quickly, they sewed the old garment together, covered the golden gown, and were gone.

When Nona awakened, she remembered nothing, but she felt a tugging at her heart and pretended it wasn't there. The tiny women of the woodwork came every night just to see her shine, but they always covered her up toward morning. Then, one night, they got careless. They were playing and having such a good time, they simply ran off when they saw the sun, so they would not be discovered. And they left Nona lying there in her sparkling gown.

When she awoke, she opened her eyes, looked down, as always, and was blinded by her own brilliance. When the Will in the Wall saw her, he too, was blinded and fell to the floor in a deep faint that lasted a thousand years. Blind and not knowing where she was going, Nona stumbled out of the World in the Wall, her whole body shaking with fear. The ten tiny women, who were watching from a place deep in the woodwork, echoed each other's plea, and ten times, they told Nona to look upwards and she would be able to see again. Slowly, Nona tilted her face toward the heavens. With great trepidation, she opened her eyes and there she saw the infinite blue of the sky and the graceful branches of tall, willowy trees reaching to touch it. And she saw that this was the first time she had ever really seen.

As she stood there, gazing at the vast openness around her, she began to breathe it in through her whole body. Soon her legs began to feel very light as if they were weightless. The billowy lightness began to fill all parts of her body until she was lifted right off the ground. Nona began to float. She let herself be lifted higher and higher. Her golden gown attracted a group of puffy clouds. These soft and weightless friends took her into their fold and taught her all there was to know about floating. Nona drifted with them for seven days, but then she began to miss the feel of the earth beneath her feet. And so she returned to her home, confident that she would be able to float whenever she wished.

From that day on, Nona remained as kind and loving as ever to others, but now there was a glow in her face, which was always tilted upwards, and a majesty in her whole being. Her sparkling gown attracted the most noble-hearted souls to her, and even when she wore garments of purple, red or yellow over it, she always knew the golden gown was underneath, even if no one else ever saw it.

♪ ♪ ♪

Working With Your Images

In your journal or on paper, write down any spontaneous images that may have arisen as you read the story. Then write down your response to the questions below:

○ What is Nona like? Draw her in your sketch pad. Draw her as she is in the beginning of the story. Then draw her after she emerges from the wall.

○ Have you ever felt like Nona? How do you respond when you feel unacknowledged? Do you get angry? Do you take it out on others? Do you confront the issue or ignore it?

○ Can you think of times in your life when you have felt yourself absorbed into the wall? Does it happen often? Only occasionally?

Only with a family member? Only with a friend, or with more than one friend? What usually precipitates it? What does it feel like?

o Have you ever felt you've given up your will to someone else? Did you feel resentful later? How did you feel about yourself afterwards? How did you feel about the other person? How could you have handled it differently?

o What do the ten tiny women of the Woodwork represent for you?

o Do you ever feel the impulse to take off the cloak of your everyday existence and reveal the unique you beneath? What kind of Self would you find under the cloak? Think back to times in your life when you truly had the cloak off. What were those times? How did you feel? What is it like to do that? What does the person below look like? Draw yourself with your own cloak off.

o List the qualities of that Self.

o How able are you to accept that person as a valid part of yourself? What blocks you from identifying with that Self? Jot down a few things that have prevented you from integrating those qualities into everyday life.

o What could you do to bring that person to the surface more often?

o When you discover the uniqueness of yourself and your strengths, how could you use them to expand your position in a business environment? In a romantic relationship?

o This power that Nona found in herself could be scary. How could you bridge the gap between your wish to express yourself and the way in which you would like to be perceived by others?

o How do you think your self-awareness could expand your emotional strength enough not to allow others to drain your energy?

o Imagine your strengths running through your mind and body, protecting you from paralyzing, negative thoughts and relationships.

Experiences

Many women have experienced very strong emotional responses to Nona's story. Therapists have found it extremely helpful for women who are working on empowerment issues. When I read this story at my women's workshops, it draws out feelings of deep sorrow, anger, fear and hope from the hearts of the women.

Many women are deeply angry with the men in their lives who have abandoned them, and with a society that subtly but incessantly treats them as if they were not important. These women seldom deal with their rage and, in many cases, are not aware of these feelings until such an experience brings them to the surface.

Interestingly enough, when I first tried the story with a group of men, there was very little emotional response. Notwithstanding the fact that it is more difficult for men to express their emotions, it seems that many of them had not had the experience of losing their identities in another person. After the story ended, they sat there with blank faces as if to say, 'What was supposed to happen?" On the other hand, I find that men who are sensitive and have integrated their feminine aspect into their lives identify with Nona's feelings of powerlessness, just as women do.

From the discussions stimulated by this story, I have learned that a great many women value themselves as they are valued by the man or men in their lives. Their own sense of themselves is often distorted and highly undervalued. If a man has abandoned them or treated them poorly, or if they have lost their sense of self in their families or through serious illness, they may subconsciously see themselves as worthless. Nona's story reminds them that their brilliance is shining inside, just waiting to be unveiled.

One of the women I worked with is a talented artist. She had studied art in Italy and her work was highly acclaimed. After she got married and had children, she put her career on hold to devote herself to her family, working on her art only sporadically. A few years later, she became chronically ill. She wrapped herself in her illness just as Nona had wrapped herself in her gray cloak. Her fear of becoming crippled for the rest of her life completely cut off her connection to her own creativity.

When she heard Nona's story, tears filled her eyes. She said, "But I **am** Nona!" Later in the story, when Nona discovers her own identity, this woman began to re-experience her own creative power through Nona. Three years after this experience, she wrote:

> *The first time I heard the story I was very sick, very depressed. It just moved me so much. The visualization was very powerful for me—I could see all the colors, and I was aware of the smallest details. I put myself right into that character. I realized how much I have to offer, when I had previously thought that with this sickness I couldn't offer much at all. The story made me aware that I really am somebody—I'm Nona in the gown. I realized that I was going to be all right. Just as Nona could float whenever she wanted to, I can do creative work whenever I feel like it.*
>
> *Remember when Nona was blinded by her own brilliance? Sometimes that happens to me. I produce something good, and for a few seconds I feel so proud of myself. I'm on top of the world.*
>
> *The story helped me realize that I can't live without being creative. How wonderful to be able to know yourself and to share your creativity with the world!*

Listening to this story assisted this talented artist in this shift in her consciousness. She has recovered from her illness and is actively working on some exciting projects. She still listens to the tape when she needs to be reminded of her brilliance. The brilliance of all of us, like Nona's gown, is just a scratch below the surface. Unmasking this secret self is the most worthwhile thing any person can do.

Music Activity #39
Music of Women Composers

Many accomplished women have not been recognized, especially in those fields which are traditionally male-dominated. For the past 300 years there have been exceptional women composers. Here are some of the better-known works by women:

Amy Beach   Grand Mass
                         Piano Music

Amy Beach	Prelude from *Suite for Two Pianos*
	Concerto for Piano and Orchestra
Lili Boulanger	*Clavieres dans le Ciel* (Song Cycle)
	Nocturne
Cecile Chaminade	*Scarf Dance*
	Serenade Espagnole for Violin and Piano
	Concertino for Flute and Orchestra
	Sonata in C minor
Fanny Mendelssohn	Piano Music
	Romances without Words
	Songs
Clara Schumann	Piano Music: Preludes and Fugues
	Romances for Violin and Piano
	Piano Trio in G minor
Taffe	*Celebration*
Ellen Zwillich	Symphony No. 1

The music of these women composers is not readily available in most record stores, but you can probably find it in your local library or you may send away for it by writing to the record companies listed in the back of the Schwann Catalog, a sourcebook of musical selections available at your local record store.

Twelve

Inner Music

The aim and final reason of all music should be nothing else but the glory of God and the refreshment of the spirit.

—J. S. Bach

Willingly or not, we are all creators, involved in the continuing creation of ourselves. Some participate more actively than others in their self-creation. But even those who deny or suppress their true nature make decisions each day that either bury it deeper or begin the process of unearthing its riches.

Once you have given expression to your inner experiences, a sense of self begins to emerge. When you deal with your own inner Nona, that unacknowledged part of you that feels gray and drab, and you allow yourself to experience the sadness of your own self-rejection rather than denying it exists, your consciousness may shift to a new place. You allow a lighter, more colorful self-image to peek through and illuminate your conscious awareness. The lightness is then sensed by those around you and you begin to feel acknowledged and respected. Ironically, it is your own self-acceptance that others reflect back to you.

As you accept your innate worthiness and the miracle of your being, you become empowered. You begin to look within for guidance and advice. Your capacity for profound insight increases. As imprisoned emotions release, your whole being fills up with joy, understanding and creativity. This process of becoming whole, which Jung calls *individuation*, leads you out of the small corner of your ego and opens up expanses of possibility. With this wider consciousness, you are able to make contact with a part of you that seems to learn and grow effortlessly.

Expressing the Divine

Heightened awareness of your own being can help you come out of yourself and your own personal concerns and connect with all humankind. Many people begin to awaken to their spiritual nature, which has been buried beneath their personas. They become aware of a deep yearning to connect with the Divine Source of all things. The beauty and depth of music gives them the gift of knowing that a higher power is always there within to provide strength and assistance whenever they need it. Once you have experienced, through music, this divine presence, you long to become part of it.

When composers are able to convey, through their music, a sense of the presence of God, they transcend their own personal consciousness and express themselves as the collective psyche. In this way, they are able to bridge the chasm between the visible, material world and the inner spiritual world. Their music becomes a link between God and humankind. When we listen to the music, we too can transcend the gap.

There is a thin line between the human and Divine when it comes to creativity. Many great composers regarded themselves as mere vehicles for bringing the creative vibration to humanity through their works of art. How some great composers were able to channel glorious music when their personal lives were in chaos and their characters less than pristine, is a grand mystery.

Western classical music began as sacred music with the Gregorian chant, and has become more humanistic and worldly with time. Many composers, however neurotic or narcissistic, were able to convey a profound sense of the spiritual and cosmic. Although Beethoven had many character flaws, his spirit was open to the music of the spheres. He felt that God was the source of his inspiration, and believed that "music is the one incorporeal entrance into the higher world." It is clear that he was aware of his mission in life. He said that music inspired one to new generative processes, and called himself "the Bacchus that presses out the wine that makes man spiritually drunken."

It seems that Mozart, too, was tapping into wellsprings of energy far beyond his personal consciousness when he wrote *The Magic Flute* and the *Requiem*. It is said that when asked how he composed, he responded, "God speaks to me and I write." With his intuitive mind, he could directly perceive the whole structure of each piece.

Although these great composers were enormously potent musical geniuses, they are not necessarily role models. Still, they are able to activate wellsprings of intuition that lead to a state of inspiration. In a 1987 lecture, psychologist Rollo May remarked that creative people have twelve times the social maladjustment of others, mainly because our society has very little reverence for the spiritual or philosophical. The personal problems of Beethoven and Mozart may have been an asset, as their frustrations with ordinary life caused them to seek refuge in the creative realms of the mind.

Many great composers devoted their lives and dedicated their works to God. Their music is imbued with great love, a spirit of service, and a purpose of uplifting the spirit. Their ability to surrender to a higher power made them clear channels for inspired works to flow through them. J. S. Bach was much more than a single individual. He was a universal personality. He saw his music as a synthesis of social and celestial harmonies. He spoke of the structure of his music as a new and beautiful social commonwealth, and as an expression of the yearning for brotherhood in the heart of man. The cosmic quality of his music reveals universal laws, and uplifts the listener to a state where she can feel the oneness of all life and rise above everything divisive.

Brahms remarked that it was a wonderful and awe-inspiring experience to be in contact with God. He wrote:

> *Very few human beings ever come into that realization, and that is why there are so few great composers... I always contemplate all this before commencing to compose.... Then I immediately feel vibrations that thrill my whole being. In this exalted state I see clearly what is obscure in my ordinary moods.*

The story is told that Schumann felt there were angels hovering around him, granting him the most beautiful revelations, which he expressed in his music. It is said that Handel believed that the music for *Messiah* had come straight from God. "God wrote it," he said, "I didn't." The spiritual purity of this music has the power to draw together entire communities. As people listen to the music, its universal nature connects their minds and hearts, melts their aggressions, hostilities, and barriers, and creates empathy.

Dvorak, whose *New World Symphony (second movement)* inspired the spiritual *Going Home*, felt that a permanent change had taken place in his soul as a result of his contact with Black culture. This music has a profound effect on the spirit.

All of these composers, and many others, poured their very essence into their music. Because they were connected to the source of all being, they were able to give to the music, and therefore to us, the very deepest expression of their own unique selves. If this essence, or energy, resonates with our own, it becomes available to us as a springboard for our own creative endeavors. Maurice Sendak, famous author of children's stories, claimed he listened exclusively to the music of Mozart as he worked on illustrations for *Outside Over There*. The music inspired him so much that he thanked Mozart by drawing an illustration in which one of the characters is wandering through a wood: "In the distance is a little cottage, and a silhouetted figure sits inside, busily writing and composing. It's Mozart working on *The Magic Flute!*"[1]

Global Connection Through Music

Aside from strengthening our self-image, encouraging us to be ourselves, and opening up a direct line to the creative heritage that is our birthright, music changes the way we look at the world. Once we can internalize, through music and imagery, our deep connection to all other human beings, we know that separateness and fragmentation are mere illusions and we begin to view humanity as an organic unit. Once we experience, in our imagery, the meeting and blending of minds and hearts, our vision becomes world-embracing. Empathy turns to caring and caring becomes compassion. Ultimately, we see ourselves as one soul in one body, created to function from our higher nature in a healthy, happy state of being.

If even one person is not functioning in a state of balance, we are all affected. The attitudes of boredom and indifference toward life are externalized in the form of escape—into drugs, alcohol, chaotic music, insipid television programs and commercials. These are the ways in which large segments of our addicted society deny their spiritual dimension. Music brings us back to the consciousness of our oneness and shows us, on a deep level, how much our progress as a human race depends on mutual love and assistance.

This shift in consciousness, the emergence of a "global brain" is, according to author Peter Russell, the greatest step in evolution since the emergence of life from inanimate matter. Just as single cells once came together to form now organisms, individual human beings will come together to form a global consciousness. He tells us that "We are all intrinsically interwoven into the fabric of the universe and are in some respects interconnected, even though appearing physically disparate." Russell envisions a worldwide transformation of the entire society.[2]

Effecting a transformation in the whole character of humankind is often preceded by a shaking up of existing conditions. The 19th century prophet/sage Baha'u'llah claimed that "The world's equilibrium hath been upset through the vibrating influence of this most great, this new *World Order*. Mankind's ordered life hath been revolutionized through the agency of this unique, this wondrous System—the like of which mortal eyes have never witnessed."[3] He is referring to a global renaissance to come; a society in which all nations, races and religions will come together, and women and men will coexist in equal partnership.

Music changes vibration and can restore balance. The heavy weight of our intellect can be balanced by the lighter spiritual energies absorbed through music. The dominator model of competition, aggression and power described by Riane Eisler in her book *The Chalice and the Blade* can be eradicated by embracing the partnership values of sensitivity, intuition and co-operation. The music of J.S. Bach, in particular, evokes these qualities.

As we resonate with the frequencies and melodic patterns of music and attune our vibrations to the common Source that binds us together, we will naturally want to choose the sounds of harmony and healing. Patterns that hold the energy to transform us are those that take us to archetypal realms where we can allow these universal images and symbols to heal, not only our individual wounds, but the wounds of the entire human race. Roberto Assagioli expressed this healing in musical terms:

> We trust that the magic of sound, scientifically applied, will contribute in ever greater measure, to the relief of human suffering, to a high development and a richer integration of the human personality, to the harmonious synthesis of all human "notes," of all group chords and melodies—until there will be the great symphony of the one humanity.[4]

As we call upon music to keep us connected with our spiritual destiny by leading us inward, our lives will begin to reflect the cosmic love and fulfillment that lies, unrecognized, in the inner realms of our souls.

Notes

1. Lanes, Selma G., *The Art of Maurice Sendak*. Abradale Press (New York), 1980, p. 229.

2. Russell, Peter, *The Global Brain*. J.P. Tarcher (Los Angeles), 1983, p. 142.

3. Esslemont, J.E., *Baha'u'llah and the New Era*. Baha'i Publishing Trust (Wilmette, IL), 1980, p. 278.

4. Assagioli, Roberto, *Psychosynthesis*. Penguin Books (New York), 1976, p. 260.

Music Imaging Activities for Children

Second Grade: Dinosaurs

Objective: To gain a deeper understanding of the size, characteristics, and living habits of dinosaurs.

Movement: Sit on the floor. Pretend you are a dinosaur. Take a deep breath. Then begin to stand up. Feel the heaviness of your body. Notice how your long tail feels. (Teacher models the slow, heavy process of getting up, along with some grunts!) Begin to walk around as a dinosaur. You are very tall. Watch out for the branches of the trees! Use your hands to keep your balance. Try walking slowly, then fast. Lean over to get a drink of water, and notice how that feels. Go back to your seat, put your head down on your desk and close your eyes.

Imagery Focus: First, let's all put on our imagination caps. Now, imagine that you are in a magic time machine and you could go back to the days when dinosaurs roamed the earth. As you come out of the time machine, look around you. Notice how the earth looks; if there are any trees or water anywhere. Pretend that there is a friendly dinosaur standing right in front of you. Notice how big he is and what color he is. Imagine that he could talk to you and show you what his life is like.

Music: Gustav Holst: *The Planets, Uranus*

Creative Link: Have the students draw a picture of their special dinosaur and their encounter with him. Afterwards, have volunteers share their drawings with the group. Instead of drawing, the children could make a clay model of their fantasy dinosaur.

Results: During the movement portion, the children had a wonderful time being dinosaurs. Some of them had difficulty keeping their eyes closed during the music. It seemed they were not comfortable being with their imaginations in the classroom. Perhaps it did not feel safe for them to enter the imaginal realm.

As the children shared their adventures with the group, I noticed that many of the dinosaurs they drew were replicas of the various dinosaurs they had been studying. There was more concern with exact replication than with exploring imaginative, original dinosaurs. However, I did feel that the children reinforced their sense of each type of dinosaur. Most of the children were not able to be very verbal in their sharing with the group, due either to inhibition or underdeveloped verbal skills. Judging from their enthusiasm and participation, I felt they had enjoyed the activity very much. I also was left with the sense that they needed more practice with free expression of imagery. The music worked very well to evoke dinosaur imagery, as there is a feeling of bigness and strength in it.

Second Grade: The Community

Objective: To internalize the feeling of being a worker in the community who provides a service.

Movement: Sit cross-legged on the floor with arms resting on legs. Bow your head, and let it hang. Imagine that you're sound asleep. Whoops! There goes your alarm clock—it's time to get up. Lean over on to your left arm and reach up as high as you can with your right arm. Stretch the muscles out. Rest it back on the leg. Lean over onto the right arm, and reach up with the left arm. Repeat on each side. Cross both arms and raise them, making a big circle as you take in a breath. As you let out your breath, the right arm comes down to rest on the right leg, and the left arm on the left leg.

Repeat the circle, and this time bring your arms down behind you, hands on the floor. Arch your back up and face your chin up to the ceiling, feeling the weight on your hands. Feel the stretch through your middle, taking in a breath. As you let out the breath, come back to a sitting position, leaving your hands in back of you. Lean your weight onto your right hand and right leg. Roll up onto your right knee and place your left foot on the floor, facing to the right at a 90 degree angle. Then stand up. Walk back to your desk and imagine you're ready to start your day.

Imagery Focus: Can you pretend that, as you get ready to start your day, you take a deep breath, and suddenly, something very strange begins to happen. You are getting taller and taller and taller. You are growing up very, very fast. And there you are—a grown-up! Imagine you could be anyone you wanted to be: a policeman, a mail carrier, a nurse, a librarian, a doctor. Make believe you can look at yourself in a mirror, and see what you look like. What does your face look like, and what color is your hair? Imagine what kind of clothes you are wearing, and what you might have on your head. Let the music tell you what your day might be like as a worker in your community, and let the music bring you a special adventure.

Music: Copland: *Appalachian Spring*

Creative Link: Have the students draw pictures of their imagery and share it with the group.

Results: Children find it exciting to see themselves as grown-ups contributing to their communities. During the sharing, they often express a sense of pride in themselves as they tak about how they look as a nurse of a mechanic and the various adventures they have as they move through a typical day. They especially feel good about helping others. It boosts their self-esteem to visualize themselves as productive, positive influences in their communities. Perhaps it gives them some hope for their future.

Music Imaging takes this social studies unit out of the realm of "other" (other people are doctors, social workers, or fire fighters, but what does that have to do with me?) and allows each child to feel an emotional connection with their own particular dreams and aspirations, to explore them and to experience their dreams as being within the realm of possibility. The music evokes a great deal of imagery, and feels like the hustle and bustle of a working day.

Third Grade: Synonyms

Objective: To understand the concept of synonyms.

Movement: Choose a partner and stand up, facing him. As you look at your partner, pretend you are looking in the mirror. Decide who will be the leader first. If you are the leader, your partner has to copy everything you do, just as if he were your reflection in the mirror. Now you are going to change your face to show your feelings. Take a deep breath or two before you change your expression. Make your face mad or angry. Your partner must copy your expression. Now make yourself look happy or glad. Now sad or unhappy. Now frightened or scared. Now switch and let your partner be the leader.

Imagery Focus: Using two identical puppets, the teacher does the following scenario, as Tricky sneaks up behind Mickey:

Hello, pal!

Hi, friend!

Did I scare you?

No, you didn't frighten me.

Then you're not angry?

No! I'm not mad.

Good. I have a present for you.

A gift for me?

Yes. It's a hat.

Oh! It's a...

Mickey cannot think of another word for hat. The teacher then asks the children if they would like to help him find another word. She tells them they may be able to find it in a mysterious place called Wordland where there is a magic machine called a synomachine:

Imagine that you could find this machine. Notice what it looks like and what color it is. Touch it and see how it feels. Can you imagine that this machine has all the words in the world inside it. All you have to do is put a word in this synomachine, and you can get another word out that means the same thing! Imagine that you could play with this machine. Let the music help you decide what to put in it and what will come out.

Music: J. S. Bach: *Little Fugue in G.*

Creative Link: Have the children draw their impressions. Mention that they may also write whatever they wish on their drawings or on the back of the paper.

Results: Children are often extremely responsive and enthusiastic with this activity. After the third grade, many children do very little drawing and free expression in class and are thrilled to be involved in this activity.

The synomachine is completely different in every drawing. Each machine is a different color, size and shape. It is striking to notice how unique each child's concept of the world really is. Often, children draw the word "hat" going into the machine and the word "cap" coming out. Teachers are amazed when children who had previously not understood the concept of syonyms are able to grasp it now. With a bilingual class, in is important to emphasize that both words need to be in the same language as children may misunderstand and write the words and the Spanish translations, such as "hat/sombrero."

After this activity, most children establish an emotional connection with the idea of synonyms that helps them gain a clearer understanding of their use. In order to further reinforce this understanding, you can initiate a discussion during the sharing to explore other synonyms with the children in an indirect, enjoyable way.

The music is very effective: the precise, structured Baroque beat gives children the feeling of a machine and helps them to think clearly and concentrate, while at the same time mobilizing their imaginations.

Fifth Grade: Capitalization

Objective: To internalize the concept of capitalization of letters.

Movement: Stand up and begin to walk as if in a procession. Breathe in with one step and out with the next. Now get down on one knee. Then stand up and raise your hands above your head. Stretch them as high as they will reach. Feel yourself growing very tall. Then open both your arms very wide and feel yourself expanding.

Imagery Focus: Imagine that you could take a magic carpet ride to the land of Punctuasia. There you meet King Capital. Imagine what he might look like. Notice the royal clothes he's wearing and what color they are. Look down and see what he has on his feet. Notice also if he is wearing anything on his head. Notice how majestically he walks. Imagine that he has a magic sceptre in his hand. As he walks through the kingdom, he names all of the people who live there and he gives them titles, too. He also names the streets, parks and buildings. Every time he names something, he taps the first letter of the name with his magic sceptre, and suddenly it becomes big and important. As you hear the music of the kingdom, let it help King Capital change ordinary things and people into capital beings.

Music: Haydn: *Trumpet Concerto in E flat major.*

Creative Link: Have the children draw on large drawing paper with crayons or pastels and suggest that they write something about the drawing on the back.

Results: Most children drew their own version of the king and his magic kingdom, tapping letters with his magic sceptre. The letters are then transformed into capital letters. The children enjoy the process of being with their imagination. They are not used to doing this in relationship to their class work. The drawings are usually imaginative and colorful. The music, with its majestic sounds, works very well.

Sixth Grade: Using Quotation Marks

Objective: To understand the use of quotation marks

Movement: Mirroring activity. Find a partner. Make various movements with different parts of your body, such as slowly raising your arms over your head. Your partner must follow you and do exactly what you do. After you have done several different movements, switch and let your partner lead.

Imagery Focus: Imagine you are a famous writer. You are going to the Kingdom of Words so you can find the most inspiring words to take back with you. You are looking for special people with very important messages. You want to take them back as a gift to your people. As you enter the Kingdom of Words, you meet the Quotation Twins, who stand guard over special words. They tell you you can take the words back, but the words must always be written down exactly as they were said, and each of them must guard the words. Then the Quotation Twins give you a little gold charm. They are magic quotation marks. Imagine that you can feel the charm in your hands.

Imagine that the first person you meet in the Kingdom of Words is George Washington. You ask him if he has any special messages for you. George says, "yes," and he claps his hands. Suddenly the Quotation Twins are standing on each side of him. They look just like quotation marks. Can you imagine them? Then George Washington says, "I cannot tell a lie." As he says the words, they appear on a beautiful banner. The Quotation Twins jump up and carry the banner at each end. Then you collect the words on your banner and put them in your writing box so you can bring them home with you. Now imagine that you can continue traveling through the Kingdom of Words, and see what other special messages you can find. They could be important words of famous people or even people you know. Let the Quotation Twins help you find them and when you come back from your trip, bring the words and your quotation charms with you. Now, invite the music into the Kingdom of Words, and let the Quotation Twins help you find the special messages you want to bring back.

Music: W. A. Mozart: *Eine Kleine Nachtmusik*

Creative Link: Have the students write about their adventures in the Kingdom of Words.

Results: This activity encourages children to be inventive and imaginative with language. Students often have personal and touching experiences. Often, disturbing emotions or impulses are released and made conscious through the music and creative writing. At the same time, almost every composition shows excellent usage of quotation marks, which may surprise the teacher. With the emotional charge of the personified "Quotation Twins" comes a wealth of knowledge and skills that have been simmering in the student's minds, just waiting to bubble up to the surface.

Sixth Grade: Drugs

Objective: To feel the difference in brain and body before and after using drugs.

Movement: Crossing one arm to the other leg keeps the brain in balance. This is called the cross crawl. Through drug use and abuse, we lose the lateralization of our brains and we can feel the imbalance.

With your body facing forward, line up your feet with your hips and shoulders. Move your head and body as one unit. Look straight ahead. Do the cross crawl (your left hand slaps your right knee as you march in place, and then your right hand slaps your left knee.) Do this a few times. Notice how good it feels. With your feet in place, move your body up and down, with your knees soft. When you sink down, let out your breath; breathe in as you come up. Continue that movement as you raise and lower your hands in front of you. Follow your hands with your eyes, keeping your eyes soft. See how far you can see your hand even through you are looking straight ahead. Repeat a few times.

Raise one arm, making a circle to one side. Repeat with the other arm to the other side. Follow the arm with your eyes, but don't move your head. Repeat a few times. Begin swaying from side to side by moving your weight first across your heels and then across your toes, around in a circle, keeping your knees soft. Reverse the direction. Repeat a few times. Then, make circles with your arms again. When you come around to the right side, your right arm goes up. The left arm goes up when you come around the left side, continuing the circles with your feet. First, everything is happening on the right side, and then on the left. You have lost the cross crawl movement. You may feel off-balance like a ship, rocking from side to side. After you experience this imbalance, go back to the cross crawl movement. Notice how it feels.

Imagery Focus: Imagine you are with some friends, playing ball. Suddenly, a multi-colored car pulls up to the sidewalk right near you. Out comes a cool-looking dude in a sharp looking outfit. It's Narco Alcapusher. Imagine what he might be wearing, and what color it is. Notice what his face looks like. Imagine how it would be to look into his eyes. Now, watch him walk right up to one of the guys. It's Robert Robot! Can you imagine what Robert Robot might look like? Narco Alcapusher pulls him aside and starts whispering something in his ear. What do you suppose he's saying? First you see Robert Robot shake his head, "no," but then Narco Alcapusher says something that changes his mind. Can you hear what he says? You watch as Narco opens his flashy jacket, and hundreds of jumping jelly beans jump out. There are little round ones, and long, skinny ones, and transparent ones filled with colored liquids. There are pink ones and red ones and green ones and blue ones. Robert Robot is so surprised that his mouth flies open and all the jumping jelly beans jump right into his mouth and down his gullet. As you begin to hear the music, let it travel with the jumping jelly beans. Imagine what changes are taking place in Robert's brain, in his body and in his feelings. Notice what it looks like inside him and how it feels.

Music: Gustav Holst: *The Planets: Mars*

Creative Link: Have the children draw pictures and encourage them to write comments either on the front or back of their papers.

Results: This activity leaves a deep impression in the minds and hearts of many children. They truly go on a journey through Robert Robot's brain and body, and do not like what they experience there. Most drawings reflect confusion. Several children have drawn Robert's brain filled with crossed wires, and written comments such as "Drugs through your veins and into your brain," or "his brain is going crazy." One child wrote the following on the back of his paper: "Robert took the pills and the pills hurt him. It was like they were alive and were eating his kidney—that's why it turned black. It hurts. Believe me, I know! He is shaking."

Peace Studies

The next two Music Imaging activities revolve around peace studies. They were designed to give children the opportunity to explore their own personal feelings about peace while in a quiet, receptive state.

Fourth Grade: Martin Luther King, Jr.

Objective: To internalize the message and essence of Martin Luther King, Jr.

Movement: Becoming aware of yourself and your body is an integral part of being at peace with yourself. Stand in place. Notice your body. Line up your feet, knees, hips and shoulders. Look down in a straight line. Position your feet as wide apart as your shoulders (your feet should be under your shoulders). Bring your head into alignment with the rest of your body. To do this, hold up a piece of hair from the back of your crown and gently pull up on it as if you are hanging from a string at the top of your head. Feel your body relaxing, so that movement becomes easy. Shift your weight from one foot across the middle onto the other foot and back again. The foot you are shifting from should feel empty. As you shift into one side, take a deep breath. Lift your empty foot. Let out your breath and bring your foot down again. Repeat this a few times. You may want to close your eyes as you do it. Now, begin to march slowly around the room in a large circle. As you march, let your breathing follow your steps. Go back to your seat and put your head down on the desk. You might want to close your eyes.

Imagery Focus: Imagine that you can see other people marching now. Imagine that it is a peace march and there's Martin Luther King, Jr., right in your neighborhood! He and his marchers are just getting ready to turn down your street. As he comes closer, notice what he looks like and how he is dressed. Watch how he responds to the people and how he feels about them. Imagine that you could look into his eyes. Notice what you see there. And now, imagine that you could magically walk into his head and see out through his eyes. As you look out through his eyes, notice the faces of the other people, and see if you can hear what they are saying to him. Notice how he responds to them and how he is feeling. When the music begins, pretend that it is accompanying Dr. King on his walk, and let the music help you find a way to be with Dr. King.

Music: Handel: *Water Music*

Creative Link: Have the children write their impressions elicited by the music.

Results: The first time I did this activity it was colored by the negative tone of the group that day. There had been several incidents on the playground where children became aggressive with each other, which resulted in anger, and then withdrawal. Many children were unable to relate to either the music or thoughts of peace. Handel's Water Music is a celebration, and did not match their mood. I have since come prepared with several different music alternatives, so as to match the children's emotional state. The response to this activity was meager, with a few exceptions, such as the composition below.

One little Vietnamese girl was truly touched by her experience with Dr. King. It seems she had an emotional connection with his essence. She wrote:

> *"Martin Luther King, Junior was looking at my eyes and he was smiling at me in the parade. I felt like he was an honest man and he was. I was marching in the parade with him and he marched with me too. He just*

came down to where I lived and then we stared at each other and moved a lot closer. I looked in his eyes and then I felt happy in my heart to see the real him. I was so sorry when he died in my street and cried and cried. I cried three hours. Before, he said, 'In my dream I dreamed that everybody's free in this city and black and white girls and boys are playing and going together on their way.'"

Sixth Grade: Feeling Connected

Movement: Form a large double circle. Find a person more or less your own height, and stand, facing that person. Connect with each other's eyes, without speaking. Move around the circle for one rotation, each going in the same direction, connecting only with the eyes. When you get back to where you started, face each other again. Begin to rotate, one circle going in one direction, and the other circle in the other direction. Look for your partner with your eyes. When you find her, face each other. Then move off in opposite directions until you meet again. Face each other and connect with your eyes again. Each pair rotates around each other, first in one direction, then in the other. Then close your eyes and rotate around each other again, without bumping into each other. When you come back to your places, open your eyes. The entire movement activity is done without words.

Imagery Focus: Imagine that you just had a fight with your brother or sister. A little while later, he or she offers to share a box of popcorn with you. Imagine that your outside voice lashes back: "I don't want any of your popcorn! If you made it, it probably tastes rotten!" You can hardly hear your inside voice, but if you listen closely, you can hear it saying, "Oh, that smells so good. I'd really like to have some of that popcorn, and be friends again." Imagine how it would be if your inside voice could come out and be friends with your outside voice. You could listen to both of them and then decide which voice says what you really want to do. As the music begins, listen to these voices, and imagine that you can hear what they are saying.

Music: Brahms: *Piano Concerto No. 2, Allegro non troppo*

Creative Link: Have the children draw their imagery, and suggest that they write some of their impressions on the back of the paper.

Results: The music, which is stormy at times, brings up a sense of conflict, and then resolves it. Most of the drawings reflected that process. Several drawings were literal examples of friends or brothers and sisters fighting, and then making up. One little girl drew many flowers that were very happy until thunder clouds covered the sky and it began to thunder. She wrote on the back of her paper that the flowers were scared and began to die. Then God saw them and brought sunshine back to them. Another drawing of flowers depicted two beautiful flowers teasing an ugly one. A third drawing showed a child running for safety into a church, while her mother ran after her. The child was saying, "Please, Jesus, don't let my mommy beat me." The title of the drawing was, "Don't Child Abuse."

The group sharing often reveals that children are able, through music and imagery, to express some of the conflicts and issues they are dealing with. Most children experience some degree of resolution.

Bibliography

Ader, Robert. "Developmental Psychoneuroimmunology." *Developmental Psychology 16 (4)*. New York: John Wiley & Sons, 1983.

Andersen, U. S. The Magic in Your Mind. North Hollywood, CA: Wilshire Book Co., 1978.

Assagioli, Roberto. *Psychosynthesis.* New York: Penguin Books, 1976.

Bachelder, Louise, Ed. *The Gift of Music.* Mt. Vernon, NY: The Peter Pauper Press, 1975.

Beaulieu, John. *Music and Sound in the Healing Arts.* Barrytown, New York: Station Hill Press, Inc., 1987.

Bloom, Pamela. "Soul Music." *New Age Journal* (March/April, 1987).

Bohm, David. *Wholeness and the Implicate Order.* London, Boston and Henley: ARK Paperbacks, 1980.

Bonny, Helen. *Facilitating GIM Sessions.* Baltimore, MD: ICM Booms, 1978.

Bonny, Helen L. "Music, The Language of Immediacy." Paper given at National Conference of Art Therapies Association, November, 1985.

Bonny, Helen L. and Savary, Louis M. *Music and Your Mind: Listening with a New Consciousness.* Port Townsend, WA: ICM Press, 1983.

Buzan, Tony. Use Both Sides of Your Brain. NY: E.P. Dutton, 1983.

Campbell, Joseph, Ed. *The Portable Jung.* NY: Penguin Books, 1976.

Capra, Fritjof. *The Turning Point: Science, Society and the Rising Culture.* New York: Bantam Books, 1983.

Chamberlain, Dr. David, "Babies Remember Their Births." *New Age Journal,* November/December 1988.

Chance, Paul, "Music Hath Charms to Soothe a Throbbing Head." *Psychology Today,* February 1987, p. 14.

Clynes, Manfred. "Music Beyond the Score." *Somatics,* Vol V, No. 1 (1984–85).

Clynes, Manfred. *Music, Mind and Brain.* Plenum Publishing Corp., 1982.

Clynes, Manfred. "On Music and Healing." Second International Symposium on Music in Medicine. Ludenscheid, West Germany, 1985.

Clynes, Manfred. *Sentics: The Touch of Emotions.* Garden City, NY: Anchor Press/Doubleday, 1978.

Diamond, John. *Your Body Doesn't Lie.* New York: Warner Books, 1980.

Diamond, John. *The Life Energy in Music,* Vol. 1. Valley Cottage, NY: Archaeus press, 1981.

Eisler, Riane. *The Chalice and the Blade.* SF, CA: Harper & Row, 1987.

Esslemont, J.E. *Baha'u'llah and the New Era.* Wilmette, IL: Baha'i Publishing Trust, 1980.

Farber, Jerry. A *Field Guide to the Aesthetic Experience.* North Hollywood, CA: Foreworks, 1982.

Funk, Joel. "Music and Fourfold Vision." *ReVision,* Volume 6, No. 1, Sp. 1983.

Gardner, Howard. *Frames of Mind.* New York: Basic Books, Inc., 1983.

Gilmore, Timothy M., Madaule, Paul, and Thompson, Billie. *About the Tomatis Method.* Toronto, Canada: The Listening Centre, 1988.

Graham, Ellen. "Retooling the Schools." *The Wall Street Journal,* 3-31-89.

Goleman, Daniel. "The Strange Agony of Success." *The New York Times.* 8-24-86.

Haas, Karl. *Inside Music.* Garden City, NY: Doubleday & Co., Inc., 1984.

Hall, Manley P. *The Therapeutic Value of Music.* Los Angeles: Philosophical Research Society, Inc., 1982.

Halpern, Steven, & Savary, Louis, *Sound Health.* Harper & Row, NY, 1985.

Hamel, Peter. *Through Music to the Self.*

Hampden-Turner, Charles. *Maps of the Mind.* NY: Collier Books, MacMillan Publishing Co., 1982.

Houston, Jean. *The Possible Human.* Los Angeles: J. P. Tarcher, Inc., 1982.

Houston, Jean. *The Search for the Beloved.* LA, CA: J. P. Tarcher, Inc., 1987.

Ingber, D., Brody, R., and Pearson, C., "Music Therapy: Tune-up for Mind and Body." *Science Digest,* January 1982, p. 78.

Johnson, Robert, *Inner Work.* New York: Harper & Row, 1986.

Jung, Carl G. *Man and His Symbols.* NY: Dell Publishing Co., 1964.

Jurisevic, Stoyan. "Releasing Emotional Blocks; The Sentic Cycles of Manfred Clynes." *Australian Wellbeing* (Sept./Oct., 1984).

Keiser, Linda H. *Conscious Listening.* Port Townsend, WA: ICM Press, 1986.

Keyes, Laurel Elizabeth. *Toning.* Marina Del Rey, CA: DeVorss & Co., 1973.

Kisly, Lorraine. "An Interview with Marion Woodman." *Parabola,* volume XII, No. 2, May 1987.

Lane, David. *Music, Mind & Self.* Bryn Mawr, PA: Theodore Presser Co., 1987.

Lanes, Selma G. *The Art of Maurice Sendak.* NY: Aberdale Press, 1980.

Latteier, Carolyn. "Music as Medicine." *Medical Self-Care* (Nov./Dec., 1985).

Leonard, George. *The Silent Pulse.* New York: Bantam Books, 1981.

Lingerman, Hal A. *The Healing Energies of Music.* Wheaton, IL: The Theosophical Publishing House, 1983.

Lingerman, Hal A. *Life Streams.* Wheaton, IL: The Theosophical Publishing House, 1988.

Lipkin, Richard. "Jarring Music Takes Toll on Mice." *Insight,* Apr 4, 1988.

Lowe, Geoff. "Music Hath Charms to Soothe a Throbbing Head." *Psychology Today,* 21 (February, 1987, 14).

Lozanov, Georgi, and Gateva, Evalina. *The Foreign Language Teacher's Suggestopedic Manual.* New York: Gordon and Breach, 1988.

Lozanov, Georgi. *Suggestology and Outlines of Suggestopedy.* New York: Gordon and Breach, 1978.

Machlis, Joseph. *The Enjoyment of Music.* New York and London: W. W. Norton & Co., 1955.

Mann, William. *James Galway's Music In Time.* New York: Harry N. Abrams, Inc., 1982.

McClellan, Randall. *The Healing Forces of Music.* Amity, New York: Amity House, Inc., 1988.

Merritt, Stephanie. *Successful, Non-Stressful Learning.* San Diego: Learning to Learn, 1986.

Miller, Alice. *The Drama of the Gifted Child.* NY: Basic Books, Inc., 1981.

Miller, Ronald S. "Reaching Our Real Potential: an Interview with Joseph Chilton Pearce." *Science of Mind,* June 1981.

Pearce, Joseph Chilton. *Magical Child Matures.* NY: E.P. Dutton, Inc., 1985.

Retallack, Dorothy. *The Sound of Music and Plants.* Santa Monica, CA: De Vorss & Co., 1973.

Rose, Colin. *Accelerated Learning.* England: Topaz Publishing Ltd., 1985.

Russell, Peter. *The Global Brain.* Los Angeles: J. P. Tarcher, Inc., 1982.

Samples, Bob. *Openmind/Wholemind.* Rolling Hills Estates, CA: Jalmar Press, 1987.

Samples, Bob. *The Metaphoric Mind.* Reading, MA: Addison-Wesley Publishing Co., 1976.

Schaef, Anne Wilson. *When Society Becomes an Addict.* San Francisco: Harper & Row, 1987.

Scofield, Michael and Teich, Mark. "Mind-Bending Music." *Health* (February, 1987).

Sessions, Roger. *The Musical Experience of Composer, Performer, Listener.* Princeton, NJ: Princeton University Press, 1971.

Singer, Jerome L. and Pope, Kenneth S., Ed. *The Power of Human Imagination.* New York and London: Plenum Press, 1978.

Summer, Lisa. *Guided Imagery and Music in the Institutional Setting.* St. Louis, MO: MMB Music, Inc., 1988.

Summer, Lisa, "Tuning Up in the Classroom with Music and Relaxation." *Journal of the Society for Accelerative Learning and Teaching, 6 (1).*

Swimme, Brian. "Do-re-mi and the Galaxy." *Creation* (July/August, 1986, Vol. 2, No. 3).

Tame, David. *The Secret Power of Music.* New York: Destiny Books, 1984.

Vaughan, Frances E. *Awakening Intuition.* Garden City, NY: Anchor Books, 1979.

Verny, Thomas, and Kelly, John, *The Secret Life of the Unborn Child.* Dell (New York), 1981.

Watson, Andrew and Drury, Nevill. *Healing Music.* Dorset, England: Prism Press, 1987.

Wein, Bibi. "Body and Soul Music." *American Health* (April, 1987).

Wilbur, Ken. *The Holographic Paradigm.* Boulder & London: Shambhala, 1982.

Zukav, Gary. *The Dancing Wu Li Masters.* Bantam: New York, 1979.

Index

Southern California Center for Music and Imagery
Workshops by Stephanie Merritt, M.A., M.S.

Stephanie Merritt is an internationally known trainer and lecturer and will make personal appearances at your business, educational or counseling site. Please check the appropriate box for information on the workshop(s).

❏ **Mind, Music and Imagery.** Experience the use of music imaging to reach creative insights, energize your mind and body, promote physical and psychological healing, and learn from an untapped source of inner wisdom. Participants will experience music imaging sessions using the Bonny Method of Guided Imagery and Music (GIM).

❏ **Finding Your Life Mission.** Designed especially for those who are considering a mid-life career change, feel burned out or stressed in your business or professional life, or would simply like to turn inward and discover what you were really meant to do. Specially selected music can help you discover your purpose, reconnecting you to your life's passion.

❏ **Finding the Inner Music of Your Soul.** Great Music reaches the depths of your soul, where you can listen to your own inner music. It opens up worlds of spiritual exploration where you can connect with your core Self and experience neglected aspects of your soul or parts of yourself you have never known. As your world begins to expand, you can call upon these rich inner resources to bring a sense of the sacred into your life.

❏ **GIM Training Program.** GIM (Guided Imagery and Music) is a music-centered transformation therapy that rapidly cuts through layers of defenses to uncover buried feelings and memories. It is a powerful tool for working more deeply with faster results. Through symbols and images, the music often brings immediate insights and healing. Introductory Level is open to all. Basic and Advanced Levels are open to mental health professionals only. Experiential and didactic presentations on the power of music to evoke images, non-ordinary states of consciousness, and guiding skills are beautifully balanced to create a life-changing experience.

To receive more information on schedules for workshops and trainings, write to:

Stephanie Merritt, M.M., M.S.
Southern California Center for Music and Imagery (SCCMI)
P. O. Box 230386, Encinitas, CA 92024
Telephone: (619) 544-0844

Other Books and Tapes
by Stephanie Merritt, M.A., M.S.
Containing Four Metaphorical Stories

❏ **Unearthing the Treasures of Your Mind** This companion cassette contains the four metaphorical stories from this book: "The Riversea Goddess," "Hoby Hyfop," "The Little Gray House," and "The Will in the Wall." Stephanie has carefully selected special music pieces to help you experience the influence of the music on the words. Each timeless story contains messages that cut through the layers of conscious defenses by using the language of the heart and emotions to reach deep within the levels of the unconscious. $12.00

❏ **Between the Heart and the Head: Stories That Heal** A special combination book and tape package of the four metaphorical stories found within the pages of this book. Teachers can use these versatile materials to enhance their curriculum. Parents may share these stories to encourage meaningful discussions with their children. Adults and discussion groups may also share these stories to discover their deepest, hidden thoughts and emotions. $38.00

Order Form
for Books and Tapes
by Stephanie Merritt, M.A., M.S.
Containing Four Metaphorical Stories

(Please print legibly)   Date _____

Name _____

Address _____

City _____ State_____ Zip _____

Phone _____

Item	Qty.	Price	Amount
Unearthing the Treasures of Your Mind (tape)		$12.00	
Between the Heart and the Head (book & tape)		$38.00	
	Subtotal		
	Calif. res. add 7.5% Sales Tax		
	Shipping		
	Grand Total		

Add for shipping:
Book Rate: $2.50 for first item, $1.00 for ea. add. item.
First Class/UPS: $4.00 for first item, $1.50 ea. add. item.
Canada/Mexico: One-and-a-half times shipping rates.
Overseas: Double shipping rates.

Check type of payment:

☐ Check enclosed

☐ Money order enclosed

Send order to:
Stephanie Merritt, M.M., M.S.
Southern California Center for
Music and Imagery (SCCMI)
PO Box 230386
Encinitas, CA 92024
Telephone: (619) 544-0844

Other Books from Aslan Publishing

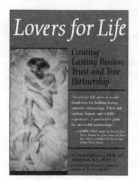

Lovers for Life
by Daniel Ellenberg, Ph.D., M.F.C.C., and Judith Bell, M.S., M.F.C.C.
Monogamy is, and always has been, a challenge. Though our culture values long-term intimate relationships, it has failed to provide the necessary tools for achieving such relationships. Taking the position that we are all beginners who lack the proper framework for creating a lasting, passionate, and loving union, Daniel Ellenberg and Judith Bell have created a straightforward and accessible guide to successful coupling—and jubilant eroticism.

The Motion Picture Prescription
by Gary Solomon
The Movie Doctor™ Gary Solomon has loved movies his whole life. He began using movies to help his clients break through their denial and heal from their individual problems. Amazed at how successful movie therapy was, he set out to research the concept and created a comprehensive data base of movies and all their healing issues. *The Motion Picture Prescription* is a helping guide to 200 movies—each one reviewed on its own page with a cast list, a synopsis, a commentary to know what to watch for, and several healing themes for personal growth.

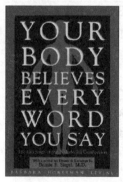

Your Body Believes Every Word You Say
by Barbara Hoberman Levine
This bestselling title describes the link between language and disease. Levine's fifteen-year battle with a huge brain tumor led her to trace common words and phrases like "that breaks my heart" and "it's a pain in the butt" back to the underlying beliefs on which they are based and the symptoms they cause. With over 45,000 copies in print, this book is on it's way to becoming one of the classics of modern healing literature.

Intuition Workout
by Nancy Rosanoff
This is a new and revised edition of the classic text on intuition. Lively and extremely practical, it is a training manual for developing your intuition into a reliable tool that can be called upon at any time—in crisis situations, for everyday problems, and in tricky business, financial, and romantic situations. Nancy Rosanoff believes that intuition is like a muscle, it needs regular exercise to be effective. Based on her more than ten years of work with ad agency executives, corporate leaders, and thousands of individuals, her techniques will help you develop your intuition into a reliable resource—one you simply can't afford to be without.

Other Books from Aslan Publishing

Remembering Your Life Before Birth
by Michael Gabriel with Marie Gabriel
This is the first book to use extensive hypnotic regression to reveal the actual experiences of individuals prior to birth. Michael Gabriel's exciting unprecedented work traces our experiences from the moment of conception through birth. It shows how deeply affected we are by our parents and the emotional harmony or confusion of adults. He offers healing processes to release the past so that we may experience joy in the present.

Magnificent Addiction
by Philip R. Kavanaugh, M.D.
This book will decisively change the way you see addictions—forever. From the unique vantage point of a physician who has treated thousands of patients with emotional disorders, yet has undergone a major life-breakdown and healing himself, this revolutionary book takes all the assumptions that our society has about diagnosis and treatment and turns them upside down. Speaking not as a detached clinical observer but as one who has gone through the painful and difficult experiences that life can bring, Dr. Kavanaugh forcefully argues for passionate addiction to life itself.

If You Want to Be Rich & Happy, Don't Go to School?
by Robert Kiyosaki
In powerful no-nonsense language, Kiyosaki shows the root fallacies on based, and demonstrates that we must make simple but radical changes in our approach if we are ever to prepare our children for the gifts of financial security and balanced, happy lives.

More Than Just Sex
by Daniel Beaver
Author and sex therapist Daniel Beaver is on a mission to help couples keep their committed long-term relationships alive and vital. *More Than Just Sex* discusses in-depth and in a lucid and candid manner common sexual difficulties that couples experience. It explores key psychological concepts and attitudes that enhance the level of sexual pleasure and intimate involvement. By giving entrance into this intimate world, secrets are revealed to allow couples to use these concepts to create exciting and fulfilling relationships. Daniel Beaver brings together a depth and breadth of authoritative information not previously available to the general public in a single source.

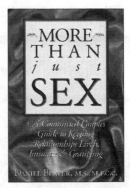

Other Books from Aslan Publishing

Man With No Name
by Wally Amos

Wally Amos, founder of the legendary (censored)* Chocolate Chip Cookie Company, started a new cookie company and then found himself the target of a lawsuit by (censored)* to prevent him from using his only real asset—his name—for business purposes. Wally Amos survived costly legal battles and confrontations with the IRS; along the way he learned the importance of strong family and community ties.

The Candida Control Cookbook
by Gail Burton

The diet that doctors recommend to patients with Candida severely restrict many of the foods that make life pleasurable—all sugars, fresh fruits, most cheeses, all alcohol and soda, mushrooms, coffee, and most flours. When Gail Burtin, a cook and former food columnist from California, learned how drastically her medical condition limited her menu options, she wrote this book to help fellow sufferers reintroduce variety and taste into their diets—without sacrificing their heath.

Argument with an Angel
by Jan Cooper

This touching, inspirational tale is a modern parable about the good within us all and how to manifest that good daily. It stands above others in the swelling "angelology" market because of its simple message of hope and the strength it endorses. The story focuses on the relationship between an angel sent to earth to round up people to make the world a better place and a young boy named Goldstein. The message is simple, poignant, and to the point! The growing numbers of "angel fans", new age readers, Christians of every variety, and teachers alike will reach for this book.

The Joyful Child
by Peggy Joy Jenkins

This book is not just for the children in your life. It is also for you. As you learn to guide your children's discovery of joy, your awareness will expand and you will grow more in touch with your own inner joy. *The Joyful Child* is both a source and a resource book. Between its covers is a wealth of ideas and activities. In addition, it is liberally sprinkled with quotations and references to lead you to a wide variety of excellent resources.

Order Form

(Please print legibly)　　　　　　　　　Date _____

Name _____

Address _____

City _____ State_____ Zip _____

Phone _____

Please send a catalog to my friend:

Name _____

Address _____

_____

Item	Qty.	Price	Amount
Lovers for Life		$13.95	
Motion Picture Prescription		$12.95	
Your Body Believes Every Word You Say		$13.95	
Intuition Workout		$10.95	
Remembering Your Life Before Birth		$9.95	
Magnificent Addiction		$12.95	
If You Want to Be Rich & Happy		$14.95	
More Than Just Sex		$12.95	
Man With No Name		$9.95	
The Candida Control Cookbook		$13.95	
Argument With An Angel		$11.95	
The Joyful Child		$16.95	

Subtotal		
Calif. res. add 7.5%　Sales Tax		
Shipping		
Grand Total		

Add for shipping:
Book Rate: $2.50 for first item, $1.00 for ea. add. item.
First Class/UPS: $4.00 for first item, $1.50 ea. add. item.
Canada/Mexico: One-and-a-half times shipping rates.
Overseas: Double shipping rates.

Check type of payment:

☐ Check or money order enclosed

☐ Visa　☐ MasterCard

Acct. # _____

Exp. Date _____

Signature _____

Send order to:
Aslan Publishing
3356 Coffey Lane
Santa Rosa, CA 95403
or call to order:
(800) 275-2606

MINMUS

Notes

Notes